Graffiti Lives

Alternative Criminology Series

General Editor: Jeff Ferrell

Pissing on Demand
Workplace Drug Testing and the Rise of the Detox Industry
Ken Tunnell

Empire of Scrounge
Inside the Urban Underground of Dumpster Diving,
Trash Picking, and Street Scavenging
Jeff Ferrell

Prison, Inc.
A Convict Exposes Life inside a Private Prison
by K.C. Carceral, edited by Thomas J. Bernard

The Terrorist Identity
Explaining the Terrorist Threat
Michael P. Arena and Bruce A. Arrigo

Terrorism as Crime
From Oklahoma City to Al-Qaeda and Beyond
Mark S. Hamm

Our Bodies, Our Crimes
The Policing of Women's Reproduction in America
Jeanne Flavin

Graffiti Lives
Beyond the Tag in New York's Urban Underground
Gregory J. Snyder

GRAFFITI LIVES

*Beyond the Tag in
New York's Urban
Underground*

Gregory J. Snyder

 **NEW YORK UNIVERSITY PRESS**
New York and London

NEW YORK UNIVERSITY PRESS
New York and London
www.nyupress.org

Unless otherwise indicated all illustrations are courtesy of the author.

Photo credits for the color insert are as follows:
SP.ONE, Williamsburg, Brooklyn, circa 1998; NOAH, Bronx, circa 1997; Freight train graffiti by COLT .45, 2006. Photograph courtesy of the artist; SENTO piece, Williamsburg Bridge, Brooklyn; REVS and COST public painting, SoHo; MQ, CLAW throw-ups, East Village, 1994; CLIF, Illustration of the page for "Art" from the author's blackbook; ESPO, Illustration of the page for "Struggle" from the author's blackbook; Collage of SoHo graffiti; PSOUP, Illustration of the page for "Criminal" from the author's blackbook; AME, Illustration for the page "Quality of Life" from the author's blackbook; AME, Illustration of the page for "Family" from the author's blackbook; ESPO, "8 Day Week," 2007; ESPO, Jerome Avenue, Bronx. Photograph © S. Powers: courtesy of the artist; ESPO, gas station, Chelsea; Black-and-white collage, Ari Forman.

Library of Congress Cataloging-in-Publication Data
Snyder, Gregory J.
Graffiti lives : beyond the tag in New York's urban underground /
Gregory J. Snyder.
p. cm. — (Alternative criminology series)
Includes bibliographical references and index.
ISBN-13: 978-0-8147-4045-3 (cl : alk. paper)
ISBN-10: 0-8147-4045-6 (cl : alk. paper)
1. Graffiti—New York (State)—New York. 2. Subculture—New York (State)—
New York. 3. Deviant behavior—New York (State)—New York.
4. New York (N.Y.)—Social life and customs. I. Title.
GT3913.N72N7   2009
306.109747'1—dc22   2008030902

New York University Press books are printed on acid-free paper,
and their binding materials are chosen for strength and durability.
We strive to use environmentally responsible suppliers and materials
to the greatest extent possible in publishing our books.

Manufactured in the United States of America
10 9 8 7 6 5 4 3 2 1

For Alma, with love and gratitude

Contents

1 Getting In

2 Getting Up

3 GETTING OUT

ACKNOWLEDGMENTS

This book would not have been possible without the support and encouragement of so many wonderful people.

Thanks to the all the graffiti writers—VERT, ESPO, AME, PSOUP, AMAZE, MEK, CRO, HUSH, RELS, KR, DES, KEST, EARSNOT, ZER, KEZAM, COLT, and others—for their teachings and for their friendships. Thanks to Alma, my wife and partner in this life, for love, patience, and enthusiasm, and for tirelessly reading drafts of this book. Thanks to my parents, Maureen and Chuck, and my brothers, Bri and Aaron, for their infinite love and unbelievable support.

Thanks to my teachers at the New School for Social Research: Terry Williams, Jeff Goldfarb, Jose Casanova, and Elzbieta Matynia. Thanks to Aaron Landsman, my oldest NYC friend and collaborator, who helped at every phase of this project, reading early drafts and indulging in intense discussions. Thanks to Dr. Carla Barrett, a fellow graduate student, who stuck it out for the long haul, for reading early drafts of this project, and for always finding me good jobs. Thanks to Desmond Hall and Adam Keene, who provide unlimited support and intense, enjoyable competition. Thanks to Niels Alpert for years of enduring friendship and raucousness. Thanks to Kareem and Jaleel Bunton, George Davoe, Dexter Samuel, Sergio Hernandez, Torbitt and Wilder Schwartz, Shannon Moore, Shan Boogie, Bob Kanuri, Brain Freeman, Beans, Louis Schwartz, Lance Carlton, Cervantes, Jamal, Jacob Waxler, and all the cats at Von and Max Fish for their constant inspiration.

Thanks to the Reverend Vince Anderson and the entire Love Choir for keeping my spirits up. This book is "Sweet Redemption."

In the past year and a half I've had the good fortune of meeting some amazing people who have been incredibly helpful. This book would not have been published without the inspiration and help of Jeff Ferrell. He scrounged this book from the publishing dumpster, confirming his belief that there is treasure where others see garbage. Ilene Kalish at New York University Press is an amazing editor whose toughness, attention to detail, and occasional praise helped to make this book so much better. Keith Hayward became a lifelong friend the moment we met. One morning he asked me a simple question and helped me to reorganize the entire text. His friendship has been a godsend. And, as the gods would have it, Tony Jefferson was teaching at John Jay in the Fall of 2007 and we became fast friends, discussing subculture theory on barstools throughout the city. Tony even edited the chapter on subculture theory in this book. I feel truly blessed to have experienced so many of these serendipitous, life-changing moments.

To my new colleagues at Baruch College, thank you for providing me a place to work and to realize possibility. I look forward to the years to come. To my students, who constantly challenge me to be my best, thank you.

Finally, a very special thanks to Stephen Powers, who believed I might have something to say from the beginning, and who was supportive and encouraging all along the way. I am forever in your debt.

PROLOGUE

It is 1:46 A.M. on a hot July night in New York City. I am standing lookout while AMAZE,[1] a graffiti writer visiting from San Francisco, paints an illegal graffiti piece. We are in a parking lot at the corner of Lafayette and Spring streets in Manhattan, across the street from a fire station. This is a relatively low risk endeavor for AMAZE. He is well hidden in the shadows and only the faint smell of aerosol and the clack-clack of the ball-bearing rattling in the metal can give him away.

I am standing next to a phone booth, pretending like I am talking; my eyes glance furtively in all directions. I am nervous about performing my job correctly. I have no ethical problems participating in this illegal activity, but I do not want to get caught. If I sense trouble I am supposed to whistle; other than that we have no plan.

Everything goes smoothly for the first five minutes, and then the fire station bursts to life. Firemen back their mammoth truck into traffic and head out quickly but silently. They stop at the light on Spring and I whistle to AMAZE to get out of sight as the firemen on the back of the truck stare at me. The light turns green and they proceed north.

AMAZE comes out from his hiding spot and continues painting. My watch says 1:57. *Hurry up.* AMAZE said his piece would take between ten and fifteen minutes and now time is passing slowly. 2:00. No cops. Cool. A homeless man looks me over as he passes by with his bottles clinking in his cart. Across the street a young white man opens the car door for his date. 2:01. Whistle. The fire truck returns and swings itself back into the station. Firemen are in the road directing traffic and they look at me strangely, trying to figure out what I'm up to. AMAZE is out of sight and his can is silent, his piece is almost finished. 2:02. The fire station garage door closes like an eyelid and the street is once again somber. The blast of aerosol joins the din of traffic as AMAZE puts the final touches on his piece. He

AMAZE, SoHo, 1997.

puts his cans in his messenger bag and we walk away, excited. When we are a respectable distance away we turn around and walk back to admire his work as if we had just come across it.

AMAZE's piece is fairly simple, with a straightforward letter design and four colors. He has used Blackberry Krylon for the body of the letters, what writers call the "fill in," which he has outlined in black, light blue, and red so it will "pop" off the wall. AMAZE is unhappy with the way the blackberry looks, but the fact that this spot is a high-traffic area will still produce the desired affect, fame.

INTRODUCTION

My initiation into the world of graffiti writers began in the fall of 1995. I remember riding my bike over the Williamsburg Bridge from Brooklyn and being overwhelmed by a large and colorful graffiti painting. The piece said "SENTO," and each letter had a different style, each twisting into the next and producing a wholeness that was readable even to my novice eyes. Various greens melded into blues, twisting back into the forest-green background, yellow highlights, orange accents, light-blue shading, and white outlined letters: S E N T O. Although I had been surrounded by graffiti in New York City this was the first time that a piece had penetrated my indifference. This was the first time I had really looked at one as something to be seen, instead of just as white noise or as trash littering the street, something to be overlooked and avoided. I related my bridge incident to a co-worker who I had overheard was involved with graffiti. He lent me his copy of the classic book *Getting Up: Subway Graffiti in New York* by Craig Castleman, which gives a descriptive history of graffiti and the young artists who created it.[1] The book told the story of one of graffiti's most colorful periods, the 1970s. I badly wanted to know more, but since then not a single text had been written about the post-subway graffiti like the piece I had seen on the bridge.[2]

I quickly became a student of graffiti. I watched the films *Style Wars* and *Wild Style* and I read the classics: *The Faith of Graffiti, Subway Art,* and *Spraycan Art.*[3] I bought a camera and started to photograph graffiti. I had lived in New York for three years, but suddenly I was in an entirely new city; it felt like the walls around me had burst to life. I began to explore my city looking at graffiti, and this gave me a greater appreciation of the diversity of its architecture and its people. I learned how to take photographs, improved my penmanship, and got into lots of fascinating conversations.

For seven years I was immersed in graffiti culture.[4] This constituted talking to writers, going on missions to watch writers paint, taking thousands of pictures of graffiti, exploring new areas of the city with writers as my guides, reading the numerous magazines devoted to the culture, and constantly reading the walls in my daily travels.[5]

I learned that graffiti is not a monolithic culture. In 1982 Castleman wrote that few generalizations could be made about the type of kid who writes graffiti, and that remains true today.[6] Writers are white-skinned, brown-skinned, light-skinned and dark-skinned; they are rich and poor, smart and dumb; most are male (more on this below); some are militantly opposed to social norms, some are quiet conformists, while others are political activists; they span a broad range of ethnic groups; they come from the cities, from the suburbs, and even from the country. They can be found in many cities, including New York, Philadelphia, Atlanta, Houston, Los Angeles, San Francisco, Washington, D.C., Paris, Berlin, Stuttgart, Amsterdam, Tokyo, Sao Paulo, and Santiago.

The culture that writers share is not bound together by appearance, language, birthplace, or class. Although many writers recognize and respect these differences, what binds them is the history of graffiti and the process of doing it. Whatever their class, race, ethnicity, religion, or age, writers define themselves not by what they look like, or what language they speak, or what clothes they wear, but by what they do.[7] Their identities are as writers first, and as members of ethnic, religious, and other subgroups second. I am not trying to claim that writers never experience or evince the racism, classism, sexism, and homophobia that are typical in our culture; but it is important to understand that these young people's identities are largely constructed from their achieved status as writers rather than from an ascribed status imposed upon them by the larger society.

Because so many misconceptions exist, it is important to have an accurate portrait of who writers are. While many of the original pioneers of the graffiti movement, like DONDI, DEZ, KASE 2, SKEME, STAN 153, STAY HIGH 149, and FUTURA, were black, in the last fifteen years graffiti writing has diminished among black kids, even as it has gained popularity among white kids. As hip hop grew and progressed many talented African-American youth chose rap over writing because of the possibility of monetary reward. However, white kids writing graffiti should not be construed as an act of cultural thievery or imitation; it is not the same as white kids playing the blues or rapping.[8] Unlike most indigenous forms of American music, graffiti is not specifically steeped in African-American cultural traditions, and white kids, black kids, brown kids, rich kids, and poor kids have all participated in the creation and perpetuation of graffiti culture from the beginning. Graffiti is rich in the cultural traditions of New York City urban youth, with kids from many backgrounds playing starring and supporting roles.

The reason that so many white kids now write graffiti does perhaps follow class lines. Graffiti is not part of the sports and entertainment industrial complex; there is no dream of huge monetary rewards that will offer a way out of impoverished circumstances. Since race continues to limit access to opportunity in this country, kids of color are more likely to be poor, and hence, more inclined to focus their talents on more lucrative endeavors such as academics, sports, or music. That is, sports and music offer a chance for the "American Dream," while graffiti does not. Athletics and rap music are at least in theory lucrative career paths. White kids practice graffiti because they can afford to do something for which the monetary rewards are not immediate. Let me be clear—I am not trying to claim graffiti for white boys, or even to suggest that white privilege does not operate in graffiti, but it is the case that this subculture is primarily a meritocracy.

However, graffiti attracts a wide range of kids because the startup costs are virtually nil. Although Jeff Ferrell claims in his book *Crimes of Style*[9] that Denver writers buy most of their paint, New York City writers are dedicated shoplifters, and the reality of race means that it is also easier for white kids to steal paint, since many store owners and security guards tend to adhere to a racist stereotype of black criminality. Writers, however, have used this to their advantage. Teams of black, white, and brown kids would enter stores together, and while owners and security guards focused their attention on the kids of color, the white kids would be stuffing their jackets and bags with paint that they would then share with their fellow writers.[10]

This is not to suggest that black kids don't have what writers call "racking" or shoplifting skills. In fact, considering the additional burden of racism, black kids must be more skilled. The first time I met a well-known black writer in a bar on the Lower East Side, he was wearing a $550 ski jacket and proudly proclaimed that he could become a professional shoplifter. Since then he has founded a graffiti collective, which writers call a "crew," starred in a documentary film, all the while using his charm and guile to "boost" or steal everything from markers and cans to jeans, North Face jackets, and even designer Prada shoes.

Race, however, can be a contributing factor in whether someone decides to become a graffiti writer. White folks do not have to weigh the issue of whether or not they will be beaten or shot by police for their misdemeanors. A Jamaican-born rapper and illustrator who calls himself Skam told me that racism was the reason he never wanted to be a graffiti writer. This was around the time when New York City police had without provocation killed an unarmed West African man named Amadou Diallo in a hail of forty-one bullets,[11] and Skam said he feared that if he was on the streets alone at night engaged in shady business the police would shoot him. As Ron K. Brunson has shown, the accumulated experiences that black males have had with the police factor into their decision-making throughout their everyday lives.[12]

Black graffiti writers, like black folk in general, have had to overcome more obstacles than their white counterparts. This is also the case for those writers who pursue post-graffiti careers. However, it would be too simplistic to suggest that white writers turn graffiti fame into monetary success while black and brown writers do not. Ambitious men and women seem to find a way to achieve their goals.

Although a minority, women have participated in writing culture since the beginning. Writers such as BARBARA AND EVA 62 were famous for tagging the Statue of Liberty, and GRAPE and STONEY were prominent in Brooklyn. PINK was one of the few female subway superstars, and her work inspired a new generation of 1990s writers, including BLUE, MUK, DONA, HOPE, JAKEE, DIVA, and SARE.[13]

While graffiti talent is not gendered, graffiti writers must literally fight for their reputations, and this turns off many women, who often choose to concentrate their efforts on legal walls. But of course there are the exceptions. PINK wrote right along with the boys during the train era in the 1980s and has achieved legendary graffiti and artistic fame. CLAW, who describes herself as a nice middle-class Jewish girl,[14] has been a dedicated street bomber (illegal graffiti writer) since the mid-1990s, with pieces, throw-ups, and tags all over the city. Today her fame is everywhere. She is the subject of a book, *Bombshell: The Life and Crimes of Claw Money*, is featured in the Doug Pray film *Infamy*, and runs her own successful line of clothing featuring her iconic claw with three fingernails.[15]

Women writers often team up with men for protection and comradeship, and this was the case with CLAW when she bombed New York City in the 1990s with MQ of DMS crew. However, more recently she has taken a young up-and-comer, MISS 17, as her partner in her PMS crew (Power,

Money, Sex). These women are no doubt tough, and while they are less likely to be roughed up or harassed by cops or male writers, women have had their share of beef. Nevertheless, women face enormous challenges negotiating dangerous streets alone at night. The street, in many ways, is a place for maleness, but these women and many like them have braved the night and demanded inclusion. While female writers have no doubt experienced sexism from their male counterparts, their accomplishments are duly noted and respect is given if they have indeed "gotten up" and are "all-city," a term used to describe writers who have saturated the city with their names.

Anyone who can get large quantities of paint, is able to fight, and is willing to break the law can become a graffiti writer. In theory, writers are not even excluded from the subculture for lack of artistic talent, what writers call "style." To be sure, novice writers with bad style and poor technique will be ridiculed by their peers, and they often quit, but with proper instruction and practice even people who cannot draw can develop an adequate tag and throw-up. When writers first start, their tags are often sketchy; but eventually, after writing their names thousands of times, they get good. The task of writing is to saturate the city with your name and any writer who does this will get fame and respect, regardless of style, race, gender, class, age, nationality, or sexuality. In its purest form, graffiti is a democratic art form that revels in the American Dream. With desire, dedication, humility, courage, toughness, and most of all hard work, anyone can potentially become a successful graffiti writer, and maybe even make a living as a result.

Illegal Writing

Graffiti, many are quick to point out, is illegal. Unlike me, not everyone sees the beauty of the form. In fact, as New York City looked to improve its image as a tourist destination and financial capital, graffiti became a target in the 1980s. Much of the effort to clamp down on graffiti writers was undergirded by the so-called "broken windows theory" first advanced by James Q. Wilson and George Kelling in a 1982 article in the *Atlantic Monthly*.[16] The New York City Police Department embraced this theory—which argues that petty crime increases the propensity for more serious criminal activity—and quickly enacted "zero tolerance" policies for many petty crimes such as graffiti writing, subway jumping, and vagrancy. Many police departments have followed New York's lead in embracing the principles and tactics of this theory in their approaches to crime control. In this view, graffiti writing is regarded as creating a visible invitation to commit further crime in a given area.

Although the broken windows theory was popular with police, and with Mayor Rudolph Giuliani's administration in particular, it has been critiqued by criminologists for the way in which it provides rhetorical justification for the harsh treatment of the homeless, poor people, petty lawbreakers, and, often enough, people of color. Cultural criminologist Jeff Ferrell describes the broken windows theory as "damn good demagoguery, assigning the blame for street crime not to poverty and marginalization, but to the poor and marginalized. A slippery piece of dishonesty, it in turn justifies the removal of such groups from the spaces they occupy, and in a still slicker trick, hides the occupied gentrification of these spaces— windows repaired, graffiti removed—inside an ideology of crime prevention and restored 'community.'"[17]

More recent scholarship has shown that "broken windows" or "quality-of-life" policing, especially with respect to misdemeanor marijuana arrests, severely and disproportionately impacts black and brown kids, who are more likely to be detained, and given harsher treatment when arrested, than their white counterparts.[18]

New York City politicians applied the broken windows theory to graffiti, arguing that graffiti not only damaged property but actually made public space more dangerous by encouraging major crimes. As a result, they were able to devote more and more resources to getting graffiti off of the subways, where it once dominated most cars. This is the argument that American studies scholar Joe Austin makes in his book *Taking the Train: How Graffiti Became an Urban Crisis in New York City*.[19]

Technically, graffiti is treated as an act of "criminal mischief" and the penalty for this oxymoron is dependent upon the "damage in dollar amount to property." While this provision speaks to the vagaries of graffiti's criminality, for the writers it can be precarious. In 2006 New York City lawmakers attempted to pass a law banning the sale of "graffiti instruments," including glass-etching cream, aerosol paint, and broad-tipped markers, to anyone under the age of twenty-one. This law was challenged in court for being too broad, and a judge eventually overturned the portion that dealt with paint and markers.[20]

Those who are caught writing graffiti are processed through Central Booking. This means anywhere from six to twenty-four hours spent sitting on a hard cement floor, followed by a monetary fine and a penalty

"Graffiti Vandalism,"
New York Police
Department reward
poster, circa 2006.

depending on, I would argue, how big a vandal or how famous the police deem you to be. The key, therefore, to being a good writer is not to get caught, but inevitably some do. Arresting young writers is thought to be a preemptive strike against future criminality. Since 2005 the NYPD has increased its anti-graffiti efforts, utilizing digital cameras and lots of manpower to track and capture "graffiti vandals." That year saw more than 2,230 graffiti arrests, a 93 percent increase over the previous year.[21]

Despite the fact that much of the allure of graffiti writing is getting away with something that is illegal, as some criminologists point out,[22] lots of graffiti is done legally with permission and, often, even compensation. In fact, the ubiquity of big and colorful murals, along with museum and gallery shows that highlight the movement's early roots and rising stars, have lately made it difficult for anti-graffiti forces to argue that all graffiti is vandalistic in nature.[23] That said, critics often focus, not on the graffiti subculture, but on more sensational topics such as gang graffiti and violence. The NYPD has recently found it necessary to remind citizens that graffiti is harmful and illegal through a campaign flyer that advertises a $500 reward and includes the tag line "Remember, Graffiti Vandalism is a Crime."

While black and brown youth in general are more likely to be stopped, harassed, or even killed as a result of mistaken identity, the special Vandal Squad detectives of the NYPD are interested in the writers who, in their terms, have done the most damage. This means that they go after the writers whose names are up the most and are hence the most famous. This is one area where race plays less of a factor in policing. Graffiti cops, for the most part, don't discriminate by race, class, or gender. In fact, for the big busts they spend their time researching and developing a profile of the writer's identity. They take photographs, scour the internet, and show up at legal spots, all in an effort to put a "government name" (slang for the name on one's birth certificate, something that many writers keep secret) to the tag. Since active writers are extremely secretive about their identities, the Vandal Squad has often made very public arrests of older writers who are transitioning out of crime and have begun to focus more on art. This was the case with ESPO, EARSNOT, REVS, and, most recently, KET, who founded *Stress Magazine* and is the publisher of From Here to Fame Books.[24]

Despite these continued pressures, graffiti subculture has flourished. From the walls of Philadelphia in the early 1960s to New York City subways in the 1970s and 1980s, to urban walls all over the world, name-based graffiti writing has persisted into the twenty-first century, and its presence continues to be part of the urban aesthetic. In a history spanning more than thirty years, graffiti writing has become a worldwide cultural phenomenon with many thousands of participants. Despite the continued public outcry and increased criminal risks, graffiti writing is an established cultural pursuit attracting hundreds of urban and suburban youths.

Even though graffiti is less visible today to those who aren't looking for it, it continues to grow and progress. While the early history of graffiti writing was documented by outsiders, now much of the growth of this culture is being documented by the writers themselves.[25] Since most graffiti paintings are eventually removed from the walls and trains of the city, writers rely on photographs to document their exploits. These photos get traded by various writers and wind up in the many magazines and websites devoted to graffiti.[26] This links writers from different cities all over the country and the world. Graffiti writers paint and publish magazines in the United States, Canada, Germany, Switzerland, the Netherlands, Australia, Japan, and South America, allowing writers to compare styles from all over the world.

The Meaning of Graffiti

Many commentators seek to explain graffiti by attempting to define its aesthetic, often treating it as a monolithic movement and characterizing writing, for example, as deviant expression, radical politics, or visual hip hop.[27] I myself first attempted to understand writing as symbolic communication. As I tested this theory of what I thought graffiti meant, however, I discovered that it meant different things to each writer. For some it was strictly art, for others a vandalistic thrill, for others a means to communicate one's worth. For some, it was an addiction, a medium that produced endorphins, but ultimately proved to be self-destructive.

Through my research, I discovered that the theoretical generalizations about the aesthetics of graffiti quickly became a moot point, as the theory could only be upheld at great cost to what writing meant to individuals. Theorizing about what graffiti pieces mean in the abstract also seemed to me to be at odds with trying to understand the critical sociological issues about who writes and how the practice of writing and the experience of the subculture community affect their lives. In other words, my training has taught me to place people before theory, to try and bring out their own voices, and to let personal narratives rather than theory drive what is put forth.

Furthermore, I owe a great debt to my graffiti teachers, who refused to let me generalize. Instead, through conversations about and exposure to so much writing, they pushed me to see graffiti for its crudeness and its complexity, its subtleties and its stupidities, its banality and its beauty, and ultimately as a medium capable of embodying contradiction. From high art to low vandalism, the graffiti writers that I know taught me to appreciate and criticize graffiti in a sophisticated fashion.

Although I greatly admire graffiti, it does not mean that my relationship to it or to the writers that do it is void of ambiguity. Let me be clear, not all graffiti is worthy of attention; like most pursuits, some of its products are great and some are awful, and this range requires seeing graffiti as a complex expression rather than a monolithic act.

However, this does not mean that there is no argument in this book about graffiti culture. Although my pursuit of thick cultural description inevitably privileges individual voices and makes it difficult to generalize about the aesthetics of graffiti writing, I still believe that it is imperative to bring out the larger sociological significance of this culture. This commitment led me to distinguish between the graffiti pieces and the people who create them, between the aesthetics of graffiti and the people who make up the culture. This approach allows me to make specific sociological conclusions about the culture itself, without imposing that theory onto the personal expressions of individuals.

One of the most exciting discoveries of this research is that many graffiti writers have found a way to make careers out of their participation in the culture. The term "deviant career" was used by sociologist Richard Lachmann in 1988 to describe the time kids spent in the service of deviance. Yet Lachmann also theorized that some of these kids who had experienced gallery success might go on to pursue careers in the arts, because graffiti writing would eventually fade away. Lachmann was correct about writers pursuing other opportunities, but the subculture of graffiti writers is still very much alive.[28] Many writers have taken their illegal youthful pursuits and turned them into legal adult careers. I will show that any understanding of contemporary subcultures must take into account the various ways in which youth subcultures have led to adult careers.

Graffiti writers do not go on to become hardened criminals, as "quality of life" advocates argue. Rather, the writers that I have known for over a decade, and so many others, have used their graffiti experience to get educations and make careers for themselves. There are a broad range of career opportunities that successful writers have forged, from professional aerosol muralists and fine artists to graphic designers and clothing designers, as well as the numerous careers within the graffiti industry, which include documenting the culture in magazines, videos, and websites or supplying a global network of writers with graffiti supplies from paint to caps to specialized inks.[29] Specifically, in the second half of this book, I will highlight the careers made by my own informants who are now very successful adults in the fields of tattooing, studio art, magazine production, journalism, and guerilla marketing.[30] But before I discuss "getting out" I'd like to talk about "getting in."

GETTING IN 1

STARTING THE BLACKBOOK

$\mathbf{I}$ met my first graffiti writer at my restaurant job in the East Village and from him was introduced to others; however, they were hesitant to talk to me. I was an outsider. I have learned from other researchers—notably, African-American scholars, postmodern theorists, cultural anthropologists, interpretive ethnographers, and feminist scholars[1]—to be extremely conscious of the power relations between researcher and informant. I have attempted to highlight these issues of self and other—or even colonizer and colonized—by calling attention to the collaboratively constructed nature of ethnographic research and the tangible research tool that I used to conduct this research.

I took my cue from Terry Williams and William Kornblum's *Uptown Kids*,[2] in which they asked Harlem teenagers to participate in determining how their voices would be presented to an outside audience. Williams recruited teens in his community and passed out journals, encouraging them to write about their lives. He called this group the Harlem Writers Crew. Williams encouraged them to write about anything they wanted, but to be prepared to come together once a week and share their writings with the group and with the two researchers. *Uptown Kids* is the story of what went on in those sessions.[3]

In order to access this world of illegal graffiti writing, I created an interactive research tool that I hoped would entice graffiti writers to express themselves in a controlled and safe environment. At the bottom of each page of a plain, black, hardbound sketchbook, which writers call a blackbook, I wrote down words that I then asked writers to represent visually in the blank space above the words. The words I chose to include came in a fit of inspiration and were based on my initial interest in the culture, which included my concerns with aesthetics (ART), vandalism (WRECK), and politics (STRUGGLE), but overall the process of choosing words was quite random. The words were as follows:

STYLE	LOVE
BOMB	ART
LAUGH	CRIMINAL
BEAUTY	1995
WRECK	FRESH
RHYTHM	SEXY
AUTHORITY	MONEY
QUALITY OF LIFE	RED
FAMILY	ADULT
CONTROL	PRIVILEGE
WHITE	EDUCATION
POWER	SUCCESS
GREED	FAME
COLOR	RISK
STRUGGLE	VANDAL
CO-EXISTENCE	MORAL
PEACE	RESPECT
1977	WOMAN
1987	MAN

Additionally, once the book was in their hands, the writers added the following words:

DEFEAT	PERFECTION
LUST	INSCRIPTION
DISHONESTY	DEFINITION
HONOR	PEN A TRAIT!
FUCK	

I was interested in how the writers would respond to this experiment and hoped that it would give them a certain amount of control in shaping the discussion. If they chose FAMILY I would ask about family and not politics, and vice versa. This established trust and led to further exploration into areas of graffiti culture that might not have been covered by a standard set of research questions.

I felt that the blackbook was the first step in building the trust necessary to form the relationships that make for good ethnographic work among illegal subcultures.[4] It immediately showed my interest in and respect for the culture as well as my commitment to finding creative ways

Illustration of the page for "White" from the author's blackbook.

of representing that culture. I created the blackbook as a way of instigating graffiti writers to communicate both visually and verbally about what they do and why they do it. The blackbook encouraged writers to show their talents legally without bastardizing the form, and it created a forum where the issues and topics for discussion could be shaped by the writers while forcing them also to be aware of an outside audience.

In addition to these more structured interviews, I spent years with writers hanging out on the streets and also doing graffiti. In these settings I often played the role of lookout and documenter, sometimes even assisting in the painting of murals.

I also used techniques of visual sociology in my research.[5] Throughout the course of this project I took thousands of pictures of graffiti. These photos, which writers call "flicks," helped me to develop a critical eye for understanding the basic forms of graffiti writing. However the photos served an even greater function. I was constantly showing my flicks to writers, who used them to judge my commitment to the culture, and these photos in turn became a teaching tool. Writers would offer critical comments about the work in my photos and would often decipher the unique styles of graffiti, which are difficult for outsiders to read.

I also started writing my own tag, GWIZ, as a way of understanding what it felt like to create an alter ego. I practiced my tags because I wanted to learn about the culture. I *thought* a lot about getting up, but actually put my name up only seven times. As GWIZ the graffiti explorer, however, I traveled all over the city on solo missions to take flicks. Over time, my knowledge of the culture grew and so did my ability to establish relationships with more established writers.

Soon, in bars over beers we would draw on cocktail napkins and scrap paper and I would write GWIZ. Writers would then write my name and advise me on my style, trying to teach me about connections, placement, repetition, and history. GWIZ became a medium for gaining insider knowledge. My contacts taught me what it takes to be a good writer, and the more I learned the more I came to respect how much work, dedication, and courage it takes to be a good writer (and also that I could never be one).

A Culture of the Moment

Graffiti culture is in a constant state of change. Tags, throw-ups, and pieces are ephemeral, and graffiti is thus a culture of the moment. Yesterday's flash in the pan has fizzled and cooled while tomorrow's "all-city bomber" is on the horizon. Most of the graffiti research that informs this text was completed by 2000, and the project of constantly updating the text with the most current writers became an unwinnable game. Therefore this text should be read historically, as a snapshot of a particular period in time.

However, this is not a history of graffiti, nor is it a survey of the best or the worst writers. The writers included in this book are the ones with whom I developed relationships. I was interested in my own generation and the future of writing culture, so I tended to engage best with the writers who were around my own age (late twenties to early thirties).[6] I found that I learned the most by developing close relationships with a few writers, which better allowed me to learn about their culture once we began to trust each other.

Graffiti writers want their names seen by writers and others so that they will be famous. Therefore writers are very serious about any opportunity to "get up." When it comes to books on graffiti, many writers only want to know who is "up" in it. This generates controversy because writers feel that being in books says something about their contribution to the culture. Many writers will likely not approve of the fact that I have included some lesser-known writers in this book. They believe it inflates reputations in ways that were not deserved. While some of the writers in this book may not have made major contributions to graffiti culture, they have made a major commitment to my understanding of it, and for that reason I am committed to them as people worthy of consideration.

This is not a book about who the best writers are simply because I don't have the authority or the knowledge to make those claims. However, there are plenty of books on the individual greats and more on the way.[7] I didn't want this text to be a survey of all-stars. I wanted it to reflect who I met and how, what they did and why.

What this book does do is provide readers with an intimate look at graffiti writing. On a theoretical level, I argue that graffiti writers can create career opportunities out of their participation in the subculture. This builds on the pioneering research on deviance first articulated by sociologist Howard Becker in the 1960s, followed by Richard Lachmann in the 1980s,[8] as well as on the work in cultural studies by members of the so-called Birmingham School in England in the 1970s.[9] Becker understood that society would label the practices of various subcultures as deviant. This suggests that the reaction to writing has as much to do with the larger sociological forces that produce theories of crime and criminality as the act of writing on public space itself. The cultural studies scholars, on the other hand, argued that subculture participation was a form of political resistance. However, since one could not make a career out of punk rock, or mod subculture, youth would be forced back into working-class drudgery. Hence, they believed that such resistance was merely symbolic.

As I will discuss in the pages ahead, there are many writers who, as adults, are making interesting and meaningful careers from their participation in illegal youth subcultures. Some would argue that those with subculture careers are simply those graffiti writers who sold out to the corporate mainstream, but I challenge that characterization. The road to an adult career is essential to any understanding of contemporary youth subcultures.

Overview of the Book

A word about the shape of the book. This book is divided into three parts. Part I, "Getting In," includes a history of the movement from its roots in the 1960s until about 1995, which is where I begin with my contacts. Part II, "Getting Up," is an ethnographic exploration of the graffiti form and the individuals who practice it. We are first introduced to VERT and the world of graffiti writers while strolling through SoHo. In "Writer's Block,"

I attempt to test my research method, the blackbook, on the street. We then meet ESPO and his highly accomplished colleagues, leading to a discussion with ESPO about his blackbook piece "STRUGGLE." Next, in "The Tunnel," I go on a graffiti adventure with VERT in an Amtrak tunnel popular with graffiti writers and homeless people. We then take a tour through the Bronx with California-born MEK, and then meet PSOUP, who did a blackbook piece for the word "CRIMINAL." I then compare the cases of legal graffiti writing with a first-hand account of illegal graffiti writing with ESPO in the Flatbush section of Brooklyn. Next comes a close personal look at AME, a thoughtful writer who built a reputation as an accomplished "bomber" during this period. Finally, I chronicle my adventures with AMAZE, a writer from San Francisco who spent his summer in New York City, and then end this part with the details of ESPO's final genius as a graffiti writer and his transition into the world of professional art.

In Part III, "Getting Out," I move away from form and style to look more closely at the culture of graffiti writers. Here I address the literature on deviance, subculture, and the emerging field of cultural criminology to establish a conceptual framework for understanding the notion of a subculture career. Finally, I highlight some of the careers that my earlier contacts have pursued into adulthood.

The chapters in this book follow a rough chronological order because, for reasons I elaborate on below, I want readers to experience the process of learning about a subculture of which they are not members. The knowledge I gained about graffiti writing was built over time. Early in the research I asked questions and made comments that strike me now as naïve. For readers unfamiliar with graffiti culture, I encourage you to read the chapters in order, as the things we learn from VERT help us to better understand ESPO and so on.

The chronology also allows readers to follow the growth of my contacts, as artists and as people, over the course of this book. The story takes place over a ten-year period in which my informants go from being kids in their twenties, struggling to find their way in life, to adults with responsibilities and careers. This is also the case for the author. When I first started this project I was much younger, and often it is difficult for me to relive the immaturity of the early chapters in this book. However, I hesitate to edit them to make myself look wiser because that was not how I presented myself to my contacts at that time. This gives the book a slightly dual quality in terms of my voice. Hopefully, careful readers will appreciate the subtle ways in which the author, like his informants, grows.

Learning the language and understanding rules of interaction are essential to any study of a group, and these were my main goals in approaching this topic. That said, asking speakers to define their terms by saying, "Hey, what does that mean?" can disrupt conversational flow and immediately signal that one is an outsider. Therefore, very often during the research I was forced to decode particular terms by trying to understand their context. This required paying very close attention, and eventually I came to understand the language and even to speak in the argot of the subculture.

I wanted to mirror in print some of the way slang is learned in everyday language. The first time I use a specific graffiti term I define it, but thereafter I use the terminology as if the reader is fluent in the language of the subculture. If you are confused, there is a glossary in the back of the book. I hope that this usage helps readers better incorporate these terms into their own speech so that they will be prepared, if not to start a dialogue with a graffiti writer should the occasion arise, at least to engage with the ideas and practices of this subculture in its own terms.

My Voice

The recognition of the role that the author plays in constructing an ethnographic narrative becomes one of the most pressing problems for those of us writing in a postmodern world. Many accept this challenge by writing self-reflexive texts that show the author as an interpreting observer finding his or her way in the field, rather than an omniscient narrator.

Susan Krieger's *Social Science and the Self* provides a workable vocabulary for the inclusion of the self in ethnographic writing.[10] She argues that any articulation of others requires a projection of self onto the social world, and therefore the reader should know how that self is presented to others. Even more simply, if the reader's knowledge is filtered through the author, the reader should know something about that author and the role that he or she plays in the field.

When I was among graffiti writers I was generally not treated as an outsider until I revealed that I did not write. Graffiti's diversity means that my white skin and style of dress did not signal that I didn't belong. In conversations with writers I would have the option to introduce myself as a sociologist doing research on graffiti. Often, however, they didn't believe me and assumed I was a writer trying to keep his identity secret. Graffiti culture's ethos of meritocracy was extended to me. I was judged by what I said and how I presented myself and my research project, and not by my appearance or dress.

I grew up in an Irish-Catholic household in Green Bay, Wisconsin. My parents moved there from Utica, New York, in 1973, when I was five years old. My dad sold life insurance and my mom stayed at home, and while they certainly encouraged my brothers and me to do well in school, we were not a family of intellectuals. In fact, my dad's working-class roots and success in business made him skeptical of intellectuals.

As an undergraduate at the University of Wisconsin–Madison I fell in with a like-minded cohort of kids who were into punk rock and the emerging hip hop scene, and this ignited an incessant intellectual curiosity. In 1992, to the surprise of my family, I decided to pursue graduate studies in New York City at the New School for Social Research.

I was never a typical candidate for graduate school. I was not an academic overachiever, nor did I have the cultural pedigree of my fellow students who were cultured urbanites who could converse effortlessly about art and philosophy. I came to the New School because I wanted to continue my intellectual journey and because it was in New York City, the birthplace of punk and hip hop. I quickly learned that I had little in common with many of my fellow students, and even less with my professors, who took my candid speech, dripping with slang, along with my newly acquired downtown hip hop style as a clear signal that I probably wasn't smart enough to be in graduate school. The chair of the department even invited me into his office to go over a paper I had written to explain to me that I couldn't write and that I should think about a different career. However, I was too stubborn to take his advice, or maybe I accepted his challenge.

I found solace in the Sociology Department and finished my liberal studies master's thesis with sociologist Jose Casanova.[11] Soon after that I found myself in an elevator with the renowned ethnographer Terry Williams. Professor Williams took an interest in me and encouraged me to do ethnographic research, and I soon became hooked. Ethnography allowed me to fuse the life I was leading in New York City—running with skaters, DJs, rappers, and rock stars—with a serious intellectual agenda that would help me to understand and explain these discrete social worlds. This all came clearly into focus the day I discovered my first graffiti piece by SENTO on the Williamsburg Bridge.

Some refer to this approach as "autoethnography," historically defined as writing about one's own culture but more recently expanded to include inscriptions of the authors' experiences in crossing cultural and emotional boundaries. Some writers who have used this method recount their own life experiences to reveal emotional worlds that were previously hidden. These tales evoke the author's experiences with difficult life moments such as abortion, death and dying of loved ones, and bulimia to name a few.[12] This method must be used carefully because it has the potential to lapse into what anthropologist George Marcus calls "mere self quests." I sincerely hope that I have avoided that trap.[13]

As noted earlier, Terry Williams encouraged me to write about my own trials in the field and to include what he called the perspective of the "I". This was inspired by sociologist John Van Maanen, who presents three genres for writing ethnography: the traditional realist tale, the confessional tale, and the impressionistic tale. The impressionistic tale is self-consciously experimental and is closest to the type of ethnographic writing I pursued. This form describes field experience, not necessarily conclusive analysis, while including the author as one of its characters. The intent is to use dramatic techniques to "imaginatively place the audience into the fieldwork situation." These tales typically allow the voices of informants to share common space with the author's. This technique forces the reader not merely to assess the data presented by the writer, but to interpret it and to form his or her own conclusions about the culture.[14]

Interactive sociologist Norman Denzin argues that twenty-first-century ethnography must deal with the complex, mediated realities of our postcolonial, postmodern, multicultural world in which the distance between guest and native, researcher and researched, first world and third world, powerful and powerless is constantly shifting. In this world, ethnographic texts are powerful commodities that shape cultural interpretations of those who read and talk about them.[15] For this reason, Denzin argues, reflexivity is imperative. Goals, motivations, and processes must be brought into the open. Unidirectional claims that argue definitively that *this* is how *they* are are simply arrogant exercises in power. These claims are especially difficult to uphold in the face of literary competition from cultural insiders who have begun telling their own stories. It is now the case that the ethnographic text and the "native" inscription sit side by side on bookstore shelves competing for readers.[16]

Moreover, Denzin encourages the incorporation of feminist standpoint critique, which questions a narrative in which gender-neutral (meaning male) selves learn from the other. Simple reflexivity doesn't solve this problem. We possess and construct hybrid identities among our national, ethnic, gendered, and racial selves, so that it is nearly impossible to say *this* is who *I* am, but rather, this is how I was at this particular time. This understanding seeks to show not only who is doing the looking, and the talking, and the writing, but that each ethnographic moment requires a projection of a *version* of one's self onto the world. When ethnographers are in the field we often look different, talk different, and act different than we do when we are playing the role of student, professor, or advisor. Ethnographers construct versions of themselves and sometimes even invent characters that they believe will be conducive to the culture under study. Although I generally revealed that I was a graduate student researching graffiti culture, this fact was usually met with surprise. As I stated earlier, throughout my late twenties and early thirties I was into the latest hip hop fashions in dressing and speaking, and this meant that I shared some common interests with graffiti writers and that my appearance was not so different from theirs. However, the version of myself that I shared with my contacts was not so different from the self I shared with the rest of the world. I did not construct an identity for the purpose of making contact with graffiti writers; however, I did eventually learn to downplay nerdy concerns with sociological theory in mixed company.

A Brief History of Graffiti Writing

The names of the earliest writers have long since faded from the walls and trains they once graced, but their contributions remain fixed as part of graffiti history. Although much work still has to be done to uncover the definitive history of writing, some elements of this history are generally agreed upon.[1] Graffiti writer, artist, and author Steve Powers writes in his book *The Art of Getting Over: Graffiti at the Millennium*, "The all city individual movement began when the spray paint markings of 'Bobby Beck in '59' began to appear all over Philadelphia highways." Powers claims that the legendary CORNBREAD, who wrote along the bus route of a girl he was interested in, followed Beck and was the first real "king" of graffiti with a reign that continued throughout the 1960s and early 1970s.[2]

In the mid-1960s educator Herbert Kohl inadvertently discovered the beginnings of writing culture in New York City. In an essay titled "Names, Graffiti and Culture," Kohl wrote that in 1967 he found that the fourteen-year-old boy he was tutoring in English was involved in a culture of teenagers who wrote their nicknames on the walls of their Washington Heights neighborhood. Although barely able to read, Johnny could read the walls and knew more than thirty names by sight. Johnny, who wrote "Johnny as Bolito," took Kohl to a wall that he says had been written on "for at least five years."[3] These writers provided the inspiration for later writers who combined a name with their street number. Writers like JULIO 204, CAY 161, LEE 163, BARBARA AND EVA 62, and so many others, wrote throughout the late 1960s and early 1970s mainly on walls in their own neighborhoods.

While these early developments are important for establishing some of the culture's roots, the modern history of writing begins with a Greek kid from Washington Heights, TAKI 183. He made it clear what writing was all about: fame. TAKI was a bike messenger who wrote his name in strategic spots in Manhattan with the intent of getting it noticed by his peers and possibly someone in the media. On July 21, 1971, he got his wish with an article in the *New York Times*. "Taki Spawns Pen Pals" showed New York youth that writing could give you a voice, and everybody knew his name.[4]

Inspired by TAKI, and spurred on by the competitive nature of urban life, the culture progressed from scribbled signatures done with magic markers to elaborate masterpieces done with multiple aerosol colors in the dark of night. A brief history of this period is best shown in photos (see, e.g., the 1984 book *Subway Art*), but quick highlights include the oft-told tale of the first piece.[5] In 1972 SUPERKOOL discovered that by attaching the fat caps from cans of spray starch to cans of spray paint, he could expand the width of the spray to cover a larger area. His signature was bigger and more stylish, and he is thus credited with inventing the first masterpiece, or "piece," for short. These first pieces were underneath the windows of the train and were called "window downs." By 1973, PHASE II, STAN 153, FLINT 707, PISTOL, RIFF, CLIFF, TRACY 168, and others had developed the piece to the point where the outsides of the trains featured fairly elegant pieces, done in bubble letters with clouds and 3-D.[6] Soon thereafter the hottest writers would paint pieces that covered an entire train, or "whole car". Many of these "burners" were done in an unreadable, intricate style called "wildstyle," a term coined by TRACY 168 and others. By 1974, BLADE was doing conceptual pieces in which an octopus held up each letter in his name. By 1977, LEE and members of his FAB 5 crew painted an entire train, ten cars, over the course of two nights. Other superstars from this period include STAY HIGH 149, HURTZ, SLUG, SLAVE, DOC, MONO, VULCAN, and BAMA.

The forms these writers executed in the dark of night were named according to the amount of the train's surface they covered: "top to bottom," "end to end," "window down," and "whole car,"[7] which referred to the size of the name.

While the reaction from the public was often positive, the reaction from City Hall was not.[8] Mayors John Lindsay and Ed Koch both implemented wars on this new form of writing to stop kids from painting on the trains. Joe Austin makes a compelling argument in his book *Taking the Train: How Graffiti Became an Urban Crisis in New York City* that this new art form was constructed as an urban problem, the eradication of which would present the perception that the politicians were back in control. Austin writes, "The new significance attributed to writing by the *Times* and some of the social control intelligentsia *demanded* that a new war on graffiti be undertaken to save the city from itself. This new framework represented the writing on the subways as a sign that the city was out of control, and that centralized authorities did not care."[9] Solving the problem of appearances then, would take precedence over actual structural changes that might reduce the conditions that produce crime.

Meanwhile, the writers of that period couldn't help but think of themselves as artists. Richard Goldstein of the *Village Voice* said so,[10] the downtown gallery owners who invited writers to do work on canvases said so, and the Europeans who were flying New York writers to Europe to paint and talk about this new urban art said so too.

During the 1980s, the second wave of superstars began to make their presence felt. SEEN, CRASH, ZEPHYR, FUTURA, DONDI, LADY PINK, QUIK, NOC, BLADE, and others added to the progression of the art form on trains, and even on canvas. At this point writing began to expand into other cities and overseas. Tourists to New York took their photos of graffiti back home and started bourgeoning movements in their cities. Gallery owners and the media also became important vehicles for disseminating writing to a larger population.[11] In 1983 Charlie Ahearn's now-classic film *Wild Style* brought graffiti, rap, and break dancing to a worldwide audience. In 1984, longtime graffiti advocates Henry Chalfant and Martha Cooper published their photographic study of graffiti *Subway Art*, allowing writers from other cities to study the work of the New York masters.

In 1985, the film *Style Wars* by Tony Silver and Henry Chalfant documented the graffiti movement on New York City trains and helped to make writers like SEEN, DEZ, CAP, MIN, and KASE 2 national stars. By 1987, as the photographs in *Spraycan Art* by Chalfant and James Prigoff revealed, the movement had become a national and international phenomenon. The book shows photos of elaborate pieces by writers from New York, Philadelphia, San Francisco, Los Angeles, Cleveland, London, Bristol, Amsterdam, Paris, Sydney, and Auckland, New Zealand.

While New York City's mayors were busy leading their war on urban youth, gallery owners at home and abroad were inviting talented writers like DONDI, ZEPHYR, PINK, CRASH, and others to exhibit their work on canvas.[12] The first gallery show was in 1978 at the Fashion Moda gallery in the Bronx. Then in the spring of 1980, ZEPHYR and FUTURA developed a relationship with an art collector named Samuel Esses. In an effort to preserve graffiti art, Esses, along with ZEPHYR and FUTURA, invited writers into his studio to do aerosol-on-canvas works. It was here that writers learned that they could successfully translate some of their creative ideas to a new medium.

This artistic and cultural explosion began to garner attention from Europeans as well. In 1983 Dutch gallery owner Yaki Kornblitt invited DONDI and others to show their work in Amsterdam. Later that year, these writers—who at home were being treated like criminals by the mayor, the police, and some in the mainstream press—showed their work at the Boymans Van Beuningen Museum in Rotterdam.

The Hip Hop Connection

Austin, an American Studies scholar, considers graffiti writing to have been the most important art movement of the latter half of the twentieth century. However, the fact remains that many scholars who have chosen to write about graffiti in the past decade have become aware of the culture through the popularity of rap music. While graffiti writers know well that graffiti was firmly established when hip hop emerged, few outside the culture understand that it was writing that laid the foundation for the youth culture that has flourished in New York City. Furthermore, it is critical to understand that writing, rapping, DJing and break dancing are linked through shared cultural traditions, rather than strict aesthetic determinants.

New York writer KET expressed some of his concerns for the ways outsiders continue to place parameters on the cultural pursuits of others. In *Elementary Magazine,* which had a brief stint as a hip hop journal in 1996-97, he said, "I listen to crazy hip hop . . . and I do graffiti, but it bugs me out that they're lumped together. When I started writing, there wasn't any rap music. The term didn't even exist and to see them placed together by people who aren't even [writing] bugs me out."[13]

BIO, a Bronx king and member of the legendary TATS CRU, is also puzzled. In *Mass Appeal* #7 (1999), when asked if graffiti was the first element of hip hop, he responded:

> Graffiti was outside of hip hop, it exists on its own. It was later on that people put it together. I don't even consider it that. There were people who were in this movement who were not into hip hop and when they started out, knew nothing about it. They were into the Grateful Dead, Led Zeppelin, Rolling Stones, and Black Sabbath. Graffiti may be part

of hip hop, but it's not an element. It is its own institution. We had so many people who were involved in [graffiti] but were not involved in hip hop, what happens to them, how do they feel?[14]

BIO's comments make it clear that there was no hip hop music in the early stages of the graffiti movement. Graffiti writers listened to rock and funk, but their tastes in music played no role in whether or not they were viewed as real writers, nor should we interpret this to mean that "punk" or "rock" are code for white, while "funk" is code for black. Writers are an inclusive, eclectic bunch who listen to all types of music, as is often reflected in their painting. SEEN, a white writer from Queens, and DONDI, a black writer from Brooklyn, both have painted famous subway cars in honor of their favorite Black Sabbath songs.[15]

Those who claim that writing is exclusively an element of hip hop culture fail to understand the history of writing culture. Graffiti clearly predates the emergence of rap music and break dancing, and I believe it would also be wrong to assume that they became fused in the mid-1970s, when early hip hop pioneers such as Kool Herc, Afrika Bambaata, Grand Wizard Theodore, and Grand Master Flash began to establish a new form of music. Although this seems to be the case for many recent scholars,[16] early commentators on graffiti writing did not classify them together. In fact, the term "hip hop" is not found in Norman Mailer's *Faith of Graffiti* (1974), Castlemans's *Getting Up* (1982), and Cooper and Chalfant's *Subway Art* (1984).

Even as hip hop was flourishing during the 1980s and 1990s, there were writers whose world views were permeated by punk rock and hardcore. In the April 1996 issue of *On the Go* magazine, REVS, a.k.a. REVLON, a superstar of the 1980s and 1990s and into the twenty-first century, writes of his early graffiti experiences:

> It's 1983. You're sitting in your room listening to [the punk band] the Necros, you take that can of "black flowmaster" [ink] and squirt it into your pinned out pilot [marker] . . . consumed with thoughts of rage and depression, you hate everything around you: the rich, the poor, cops, blue collar guys, girls, yourself and even God. Your only undying gratitude is toward graffiti and punk rock, two venues where you can express your disdain.[17]

I do not want to diminish the enormous significance of hip hop culture, only to emphasize the critical role graffiti played in the emergence of

Los Angeles gang writing. "QUATRO FLATS" mark their turf by crossing out rivals. Photograph courtesy of COLT .45.

youth cultures. From the start, writers referred to themselves as "writers." The term "graffiti," which connotes vandalism and witticisms on the bathroom wall, served those who wished to influence public opinion about the culture and its practitioners. Writers used this term until the late 1990s, when it became a subject of controversy in the community.[18] While many writers eschewed the term, others have chosen to continue to use "graffiti" even after the recognition that it was a label affixed by outsiders. When I hear writers use the term "graffiti" or "graff," I interpret it as a conscious choice to reclaim the term in a positive sense.

Scholars began to use the term "hip hop graffiti" when rap trickled up into the academy. While I must admit this term does separate name-based writing culture from sloganeering or gang writing, the aesthetics of these three forms are easily distinguishable. Political writing tends to be spontaneous and lacks a certain calligraphic style, while gang writings, or "placas," are boxy line signatures that announce gang territory and not necessarily the name of the writer.[19]

The term "hip hop graffiti" is also problematic because writers themselves never use it; it reveals an ignorance of the cultural and historical roots of writing culture. In a 1990 article, ethnographic researchers Devon D. Brewer and Marc L. Miller distinguished between what they call New York City's independent graffiti history and the cultures that developed in other cities on the basis of hip hop. They argue that hip hop culture was the vehicle for graffiti's national and worldwide explosion, and hence all

West Coast writers identify themselves with the "3 pillared hip hop sub-culture of rap music, breakdancing and graffiti."[20]

Certainly hip hop culture, and especially the efforts of organizations like the Zulu Nation and break dancers such as the Rock Steady Crew,[21] was integral in disseminating writing to a larger worldwide audience. Yet other cultural elements were also responsible for its popularity. There were writers in the early 1980s who identified with punk and hardcore (and hip hop) and hence brought writing with them when they traveled with bands to other cities or exchanged self-produced fanzines.[22]

Brewer and Miller's claim that all West Coast writers identify with hip hop also is not correct. Many writers in Los Angeles and especially San Francisco identify more closely with punk and hardcore. Graffiti writers listen to a wide variety of musical genres, including but not limited to rap. Current writers such as TWIST, AMAZE, PEZ, and others continue to show this diversity.

It is important to note, however, that this cultural diversity is not a question of racial demarcation. Graffiti has always been and continues to be a racially, ethnically, and economically diverse culture. Writing is a meritocracy; it's about skills. It should not be construed that there are status divisions between the writers who are into hip hop and those who are drawn to other types of music. Hip hop and graffiti are related cultural phenomena with complex histories, but there are no strict aesthetic formulae that connect them.

Jeff Ferrell's innovative work of criminology, *Crimes of Style: Urban Graffiti and the Politics of Criminality*, deals with the historical problem of hip hop and graffiti in a unique way. While mentioning the pioneering efforts of TAKI and JULIO, who predate hip hop, Ferrell argues that it wasn't until "style became a way of distinguishing the name that hip hop graffiti began to emerge."[23] Ferrell essentially argues that there are two cultures, graffiti and hip hop graffiti, with style being the dividing line. For commentators like Ferrell, graffiti becomes worthy of serious attention when pieces have progressed to a level at which outsiders can appreciate their artistic power. But even this assumption is incorrect because the style that Ferrell is talking about was clearly established by 1973–74, which still predates hip hop.

Susan Phillips, author of *Wallbangin'*, is another scholar who uses the term "hip hop graffiti." For Phillips the term is necessary to distinguish that form of graffiti from the writing that gangs employ. However, this confusion is cleared up if we insist that we are talking about writing culture.

Gangs write to advertise and to demarcate space, but writing certainly is not the main purpose for their cultural cohesion.

Phillips also has her history backwards. She writes, "Hip hop graffiti evolved in the frenetic urban environment of 1970s New York City where it was an aspect of the generalized hip hop culture that included rap music, break dancing and advanced graffiti stylings."[24] Once again we see an argument that writing is rooted in a culture that did not exist at the time.

Those who use the term "hip hop graffiti" should understand that this label is two levels of abstraction away from how writers themselves refer to their activity. Not only is the label not embraced by the community, but it also speaks to a misunderstanding of the history and culture of both writing and hip hop. Correcting these historical inaccuracies is necessary to increase rather than frustrate our appreciation for the complex ways that graffiti and hip hop forms are linked.

While many scholars have their hip hop wrong, there have been some very good books on graffiti culture. Three important ethnographies of graffiti have been published since the movement began more than thirty years ago. Craig Castleman's *Getting Up* (1982) remains seminal in its exploration of the train era, while Jeff Ferrell's *Crimes of Style* (1996) explores the graffiti scene in Denver. In his closing chapter Ferrell develops a theory of criminology that proposes that graffiti inspires hatred by conservative moral entrepreneurs because it upsets the "aesthetics of authority" embedded in a clean wall that is meant to inspire order. These ideas would lay the groundwork for the emerging field of cultural criminology.[25] Nancy McDonald's *The Graffiti Subculture* (2001) is the first truly global graffiti book, looking at subcultures in New York and London. Her book offers detailed depictions of the culture and an excellent theoretical criticism of the Birmingham School. However, her main premise—that graffiti is a site for the formation of male identity—leaves out women and operates under the influence of stereotypes about masculinity. Further, she makes no distinction as to why graffiti is any different from any other male adolescent pursuit, such as football or the chess club.

As mentioned, Joe Austin's *Taking the Train* (2001) is a historical account of the construction of graffiti as a crime in New York City. It shows how politicians' media campaigns played on racist fears of urban youth to construct graffiti as a symbol of the city's woes. Thus, cleaning up the city meant waging a "war" against some of its most talented teenagers. These tactics marked the beginning of policies that battle the perception of crime rather than actual crime.

Ivor Miller's *Aerosol Kingdom* (2002) offers a reflexive interpretation of the cultural roots of graffiti. Miller seeks to show cultural continuity between the West African *orisha* Ogun—the god of iron—and African-, Caribbean-, and Puerto Rican–American youths' application of aerosol to the steel sides of subway cars. Throughout the course of the book, Miller backs away from his central argument and lets the writers' voices carry the text; however, it remains unclear how he accounts for the fact that graffiti began on cement walls and continues to thrive without iron.

From the Windows to the Walls

The graffiti movement's train era officially came to a close in 1989, when city officials began refusing to put painted trains into service. The subways could no longer be used as a medium of communication, and writers stopped painting exclusively on trains because they no longer provided a pathway to fame.

The movement found a new medium. Photographs of graffiti made permanent what is essentially ephemeral, allowing writers to view the work of others without attachment to a specific place or time. The inclusion of flicks in magazines created a space where graffiti pieces from all over the world ran together to be judged, critiqued, and learned from. This liberation of graffiti from a geographically specific location essentially formed the beginnings of a global community of writers.

The transition from moving underground trains to walls all over the city and later the world is a significant development that gets scant attention. Many observers and even practitioners of the culture see this shift as the beginning of a slow decline from the early heyday of the movement. While not wanting to diminish the movement's brilliant beginnings, the end of the train era also freed writers from underground tunnels and turned them into experts of urban exploration in cities all over the world.

During the early train era in New York, a writer's worldview consisted of miles of underground tunnels. As writers gained knowledge and experience, their conception of their world changed, as did their goals—from all-city to all-world. Today, significant graffiti writing scenes can be found in almost every major world city, and yet they are not insular. Many of today's top writers have traveled to cities around the world to paint, while even more have made the pilgrimage to New York, the mecca for writers everywhere. This transition from city-wide fame to national, and eventually

Freight train graffiti by COLT .45, 2006. Photograph courtesy of the artist.

international, stardom was further assisted by writers who began painting outbound freight trains.[26] While this development helped send various cities' graffiti images out to a nationwide audience, most New York City writers became familiar with writers in other cities through photographs, magazines, and personal travel.

The 1990s saw a resurgence among writers who began their careers on subway steel but quickly came aboveground and were among the first to be "all-city" on walls. JOZ, EASY, JOSH 5, SMITHSANE, JA, REVS, COPE, and VFR are some of the undisputed kings of this era.[27] Since the train no longer provided a single frame of reference, these writers rarely used specific terms to denote the size of their work. The focus became how the surface was covered rather than how much. Contemporary post-subway graffiti writing occurs in three main forms: the tag, the throw-up, and the piece.[28] Although all three forms are means to explore the letters in a name, each has its own specific critical criteria.

Piece, short for masterpiece, is the term for a colorful mural. A throw-up is usually painted with an outline color and a fill-in color and is also called a "fill-in." The third type of graffiti, the tag, consists of the writer's signature done with marker or paint. Of these three, the piece is arguably the most complicated writing craft, utilizing three dimensions and numerous colors. However, even writers who learn the art of piecing continue to develop their tags and throw-ups, constantly exploring different approaches to letters. But before writers begin to explore their individual styles in these forms, they must choose a name.

Graffiti is the public application of an alias for the purpose of fame. Fame is based on saturation and style, and choosing a name for oneself is the first element of style. Writers also choose their names based on practical considerations. More letters take more time, so the most prolific writers, or kings, have two- or three-letter names, although there are exceptions. Writers also will often change names throughout their careers. Many writers' first graffiti names are chosen spontaneously and without much thought; as they learn more about doing graffiti, and about themselves, they will choose a name that really fits their style. Writers will also develop additional aliases to experiment with other letters, to inject some mystery and intrigue, to signify a change in approach, to explore other characters, or to remain incognito to thwart cops and competitors. However, each name, regardless of its prior meaning, is a clean slate. The meaning the name takes on is created by the writer's deeds. This is manifested in the writer's pieces, tags, and throw-ups.

PINK, Williamsburg, Brooklyn, circa 1996.

CASE 2, Harlem, 1998.

NOAH, Bronx, circa 1997.

SP.ONE, Williamsburg, Brooklyn, circa 1998.

PIECES

Pieces are big and beautiful. This is the form in which writers release the full onslaught of their stylistic power. Artists utilize multiple paint colors and complex letter construction, as well as characters and designs. Intricate, unreadable styles are called "wildstyle" pieces, and the ones that are extremely hot are called "burners." Today, so many kids paint "wildstyle burners" that it is almost a style unto itself.[29]

Aerosol paint is difficult to master and requires an enormous amount of practice to achieve the necessary technical sophistication to paint smooth, clean lines. Unlike other visual artists who have an almost unlimited number of brushes to apply color to a surface, a graffiti writer has only a limited array of "fat" and "skinny" "caps" to vary the width of the spray.[30] Other variants of width and shade must be achieved by intricate finger maneuvers and tilting of the can. Writers call this having "can control." Can control isn't only drip prevention; it is a learned technique that requires precise coordination in order to place the desired width of paint cleanly on a surface.

Pieces are the least controversial form of graffiti writing. Even those who are adamant that graffiti is criminal often cannot help but appreciate pieces as art.[31] This mainstream acceptance of graffiti murals has led some entrepreneurs and community activists to open legal graffiti spots. In doing so, they produce all the right rhetoric for giving kids a chance and allowing them to progress artistically, as well as keeping them, and their graffiti, off of the streets. More recently, corporations such as Ecko and Adidas have garnered attention for hosting legal graffiti events, and City Councilman Peter Vallone, Jr., never misses an opportunity to get himself in the newspaper decrying such events for promoting crime.

The prevalence of legal graffiti spots in cities all over the world, combined with the World Wide Web, has added another path to fame that doesn't include illegally saturating city walls with a name. Many writers only paint legal walls and send the photos to the numerous graffiti websites. Kids who want to see graffiti turn on their computers and scroll through flicks from the top writers from around the world. The really hot pieces create a buzz, and some writers are then invited to go to the various legal wall spots all over the world. For the top muralists there is a sort of graffiti circuit that includes spots in Queens, Minneapolis, Chicago, Cincinnati, Los Angeles, San Francisco, Tokyo, Australia, New Zealand, Barcelona, Madrid, Munich, and Copenhagen, to name a few.

Writers use the Web the same way they used other media—to promote themselves. The Web provides a sense of public anonymity that graffiti writers have long capitalized on. Many crews have their own websites. Writers have blogs and MySpace pages and also use photography and video sites like Flickr and YouTube to show off their latest exploits.

While the execution of tags and throw-ups has remained relatively unchanged over the years, the piece is now very different from its historical roots—not speaking in terms of aesthetics, but of context. Legal pieces are executed under the best possible circumstances, while writers who painted (and invented) pieces on trains did so in the harshest of environments. It

REVS and AMAZE roller tags, SoHo, 1998.

REVS:COST roller tags, Upper West Side, entrance to the Freedom Tunnel.

was dark and cold and the threat from the police and even other writers was imminent. These adventurous pioneers culled all of their creativity and exploded it onto a subway car in a short amount of time, and then, as the sun was coming up, hobbled into a train station to see how their work looked in the morning light.

Today's celebrity writers paint elaborate, perfect, mind-blowing productions on sunny afternoons, sometimes taking two days to finish. The

REVS and COST public painting, SoHo.

COLT .45 roller piece, Bronx.

pressure they experience comes from their own desire to push themselves creatively, as well as the expectations that come with fame. They have to do their best work with gawkers and autograph-seekers wanting their attention and causing constant distractions.

Yet, writers continue to find spots to piece illegally, as well as developing other forms for getting up big. COST and REVS pioneered the process of using buckets of paint with rollers on extended poles to paint

SOME and KR hangover piece, Chinatown, circa 2000.

their names huge in high-up, prominent places. These enormous pieces—often called "roller tags"—evoke the same sort of how-the-hell-did-they-do-that awe of the train era. Over the last few years these pieces have even developed stylistically, as writers have become more proficient with the rollers.

One new technique with rollers results in what is called a "hangover piece." The writer stands on the roof and paints the piece upside down while hanging over the wall. KR, SOME, and others have perfected this technique, painting cleanly and with multiple colors, showing once again that you can create art with a tool designed for the practical purpose of covering surfaces.

COST and REVS complemented their roller tags with an onslaught of 8.5" x 11" posters that they pasted all over the city. Using wheat paste and "official"-looking uniforms, COST and REVS affixed posters with their names on them on the back of almost every "walk/don't walk" sign in the city.

Their efforts at expanding the means for getting up also included studio paintings on huge metal canvases that they then bolted to the sides of buildings. In the last half-decade REVS has been making iron sculptures in his studio and then welding them in public spots, offering his own version of public art. And he has continued to paint his underground autobiography in each tunnel in the subway system.[32]

THROW-UPS

Ultra-detailed pieces painstakingly painted, are products of a permissive environment, black and white are the colors of speed and illegal deeds.[33]

—Espoet, *On the Go #10*

Throw-ups are easy to distinguish from the colorful pieces because they
are most often done in only two colors and in "bubble" letter style. Originally a term for a poorly done piece—something just "thrown up" on the
train without much effort or style—the throw-up was the last of the three
forms of writing to evolve. As available space on trains decreased, the

MQ, CLAW throw-ups, East Village, 1994.

JA KEZ throw-ups, Lower East Side, circa 1998.

competition increased considerably. Some writers concentrated purely on saturation techniques, and some crews developed strategies for taking over entire train lines by saturating the train with a quickly executed name.

One story has it that around 1974–75, IN and his T.O.P. crew mates were among the first to take the name out of its piecework days and into mass production. IN, along with ON, OI, and others, had a plan to paint quick two-color pieces on every car in a line in order to become kings in a relatively short period. By utilizing two colors and a bubble letter style they could get up with extreme speed and take over enormous amounts of space. According to Castleman, IN numbered his throw-ups and quit when he reached five thousand. Other writers quickly realized that they could mass-produce their names and rapidly increase the currency of their fame. The throw-up became one of the fundamental techniques for getting up, and thereby gaining recognition and fame. This also began the rough line of demarcation within the culture between piecers and bombers, whose main interest is saturation rather than style.[34]

Most sociologists studying graffiti culture believe that there is a status division between the "crude" bombers and the "pretty" piecers. The first division among writers, however, is between "toys," or neophytes, and masters. It is incorrect to say that toys tag and masters piece; toys just do bad tags, bad throw-ups, and bad pieces. Although many writers lack the skill or desire to become style masters, bombers perfect their tags and throw-ups for speed and efficiency as they saturate the entire city. It is wrong to assume that writers who just get up are not respected by their peers, or that their throw-ups or tags show no style; in many ways it is the bombers, not the style masters who do legal walls, who are the true superstars of this culture.

Throw-ups are done with a dark outline color and a lighter fill-in color. The throw-up is executed with incredible speed and almost always at night. To perform a throw-up a writer first makes an outline with the lighter color and fills it in; then a second outline is made on top with the darker color. Precision of movement and control of the paint can are crucial to skillful throw-ups. They require a surprisingly physical performance; writers must throw their whole bodies into the piece with sweeping arm movements that must be coordinated with their legs. In order to achieve clean lines, the writer must move laterally along the wall to keep the flow of paint even and consistent. The physical element of throw-ups brings together some of the athletic and artistic elements of graffiti. ESPO likes to say that doing throw-ups is a "graffiti workout."

Throw-ups are done on illegal walls so there is no time for the intricate maneuvers involved in piecing. In this case, style follows function, and the function of the throw-up is to be up; thus a good throw-up style is one that can be executed quickly. The need for speed gives some insight into throw-up style. The throw-up is mastered by painting smooth, flowing lines. This requires writers to think of the whole word rather than its individual letters.

Today's fill-ins have a wholeness to them that often makes them difficult to read. A throw-up is recognizable by its overall shape and with repetition becomes an icon for a writers' name.

TAGS

The tag is the most frequently executed of all the forms of graffiti. The tag is small and is considered a writer's signature. It can be done with a multitude of mediums, including wide felt-tip markers, paint pens, spray paint, and other creative household items such as shoe polish bottles filled with industrial ink[35] and markers made from chalkboard erasers stuffed into roll-on deodorant bottles. Writers call these homemade marking tools "mops."[36]

Tagging is the form in which regional differences in style are most clearly noted. Philly signatures go back the furthest and have their own

TWIST and AMAZE tags, SoHo, 1996.

SEN4, NYMZ, and VFRESH tags, East Village.

EARSNOT tag, Chelsea.

indigenous history that was not imported from New York. Philly writers have different styles of prints for different functions: "tall" prints work well on doors; "rally" prints, which is the name written over and over again, are used to cover lots of space (as opposed to New York writers, who add letters to their names); and "wickets," or "wickeds," are a complex writing style that has a rhythmic requirement of eight beats per letter.[37]

Los Angeles has its own style, "cholo marking" or "placas," which is rooted in Mexican culture and dates back to the 1930s; this style flourished during the height of the Zoot-suiters in the 1950s. These markings have a specific aesthetic form and are used to promote a gang and its members. Although this style has evolved into an art form, as evidenced by the work of artist Charles "CHAZ" Bojorquez, it is a separate culture from the name- and fame-based graffiti.[38] Los Angeles writing styles have both gang and New York City influences. San Francisco also has a stylistic history that is fairly discernible; however, transplanted New York writers—most notably KR—have had a huge impact on that city's writing style.

Gallery Redux

The public's appetite for graffiti soured in the early 1990s, and the gallery opportunities for American writers also fizzled. Successful illegal graffiti artists in the early 1990s no longer had opportunities to become professional artists right out of high school, so many put together portfolios of their graffiti work and got accepted to art schools. There they used the institutions' facilities to learn fine art, graphic design, photography, video editing, and filmmaking. These skill sets would eventually help writers to produce professional-looking graffiti magazines, videos, and websites.

The idea of graffiti names painted on canvas lost much of its momentum, but in the mid-1990s the next generation of writers, many of whom were art school graduates, forced their way back into galleries to do installations. TWIST, also known as Barry McGee, was a pioneer of this direction and his success created opportunities for others. Fellow former writers Steve Powers, Todd James, and many others have moved beyond piecing with spray cans to conceptual pieces that deal with signage, commercialism, fame, and urban aesthetics. This artistic work is not graffiti, but it is clear by their use of letters, graphics, and sometimes aerosol paint, that each of these artists' visions was developed in conversation with the city's built environment.

As graffiti writers get older they tend to do less illegal writing, but they remain members of the subculture. Some of the most talented turn their vision toward a career in the art world, and there are also writers who have turned their youthful graffiti success into adult careers as muralists for hire, tattoo artists, graphic designers, and magazine publishers. While still reviled and misunderstood by many in the mainstream, graffiti style has also found its way into popular culture, creating further opportunities for former graffiti writers. Corporate advertisers and TV shows use and sometimes abuse graffiti as an icon of urban cool. Writers have painted backdrops for films, done advertising murals for Coke, and designed sneakers.[39]

Criminologists who study how we age—or what we refer to as the "life course"—suggest that it is quite normal for young people to cease criminal activity as they get older.[40] In fact, research shows that "desisting" petty crimes like binge drinking, illicit drug use, and shoplifting is indeed, along with finding a job, a marker of adulthood.[41] My research confirms that graffiti writers, like many young people, moderate their deviance as they approach adulthood and believe, like most folks, that a career, a steady income, a spouse and a family are all symbols of adulthood. For many writers, however, their ability to achieve these successes is directly dependent upon their participation in an illegal subculture. Graffiti writers who have built a reputation and have avoided (for the most part) arrest find that as they age they have the option of using their talent, knowledge, and fame to transition into an adult career. While those who study "desistance," or the opting out of crime, make clear that most young people turn away from crime as they approach their thirties and instead "settle down" into adult roles, none of the research can account for the fact that participation in an illegal subculture nurtured their talents and helped them to find careers in the first place.

Cultural criminologists understand that many criminal subcultures engage in what Ferrell calls "crimes of style." Young people's activities are criminalized as much for their aesthetics—think Elvis, punk rock, rap, graffiti writing—as for their supposed vandalism or transgressive sexuality.[42] The criminality of these acts is imbedded in a set of cultural practices that often require a coordinated media and public relations campaign to force the public to see certain acts as serious crimes rather than artistic expressions. Graffiti, however, confounds these binaries; it is legal and illegal, crime and art, vandalism and community service. This is one of the key components to understanding how one can make a career as a graffiti writer. As some writers age they do graffiti more as art and less as crime. This marks a unique relationship between crime and the various paths to adulthood.[43] It would be akin to drug dealers using their knowledge of chemistry to get into college and then becoming professional pharmacists. Graffiti writers engaged in a set of activities as young people that police and politicians insisted were harmful to society. However, rather than moving on to more serious forms of criminal activity, many graffiti writers forged a path to legitimate adult success.

Despite these tendencies toward legitimate careers and opportunities for selling out, street bombers continue to make their mark. Some current stars like EARSNOT, DASH, SACER, DRO, and 2EASAE have inspired a whole new generation of writers who, like those before them, continue to explore the boundaries of expression in urban space.

CRIME SPACE VS. COOL SPACE
Breaking Down Broken Windows

Since its beginning in the late 1960s to its heyday on the subways of New York City, graffiti writing has been a contentious and controversial art form. Today many in the mainstream have come to accept colorful graffiti murals, or pieces, as part of pop culture. However, even for those who appreciate graffiti pieces for their artistic merit, the lowly signature or tag remains reviled.

There seems to be a consensus in the mainstream that graffiti murals are art while tags are just vandalism. Within graffiti culture itself, however, no such strict division exists between the various forms of contemporary graffiti. Pieces, throw-ups, and tags are all ways in which writers attempt to get their name seen for the purpose of achieving fame. Anti-graffiti

SENTO tag, East Village.

SENTO piece, Williamsburg Bridge, Brooklyn.

advocates attempt to separate the tag from the other forms of graffiti by arguing that tags can never be art, only vandalism. But just because tags are illegal does not mean that they have no aesthetic appeal or that some tags aren't better than others. Writers practice their tags, or "handstyles," constantly and put lots of thought and energy into figuring out the best spots to put their names up.

The insistence that illegal graffiti writing is just petty vandalism has been undergirded by the "broken windows theory" advanced by Wilson and Kelling in the early 1980s. Since this theory has been so influential in contemporary policing in New York City and throughout the nation, it is worth investigating a bit more here. To recap, Wilson and Kelling argue that signs of disorder such as broken windows are a signal to criminals that "no one cares" about maintaining order, and that this is thus a space in which to commit crime.[1] In New York City, police and politicians have applied this to graffiti by arguing that although it may be a minor crime, it acts as an invitation for major crimes to occur. In fact, they argue that graffiti not only damages property but actually makes public space more dangerous by turning neutral space into crime space.

As applied to policing, "broken windows theory" argues that rooting out "signs of disorder" can lead to less lawbreaking. These signs of disorder, like broken windows, vagrancy, and littering, however, are more likely to occur in poor neighborhoods. That being the case, so-called "quality of life" policing quickly becomes a justification for police occupation of poor communities and harsh treatment of the people living in these neighborhoods. A recent study by criminologists Bernard Harcourt and Jens Ludwig has shown that "quality of life policing," especially with respect to misdemeanor marijuana arrests, severely impacts black and brown kids, who are more likely to be detained, more likely to be given harsher treatment, and more likely to be arrested than their white counterparts.[2] An exhaustive quantitative study by legal scholars Jeffrey Fagan and Fritz Davis has shown that race is the primary indicator in "stop and frisk" procedures—which, though they may be successful in getting guns off the street, are viewed by many as a form of harassment. Fagan and Davis conclude, "Our empirical evidence suggests that policing is not about disorderly places, nor about improving quality of life, but about policing poor people in poor places."[3] Andrew Karmen, in his book *New York Murder Mystery*, has also exploded the myth of the success of "quality of life" policing in reducing crime.[4] Despite these studies contradicting its effectiveness, "broken windows" policing largely remains the law of the land.

Graffiti writing, however, is different from other "quality of life" crimes, because it does not exist exclusively or even primarily in poor neighborhoods. Graffiti writers write in order to get fame and respect for their deeds, and therefore they write in places where their work is more likely to be seen by their intended demographic. It is not the amount of disorder that determines a good spot to write graffiti, but the number of potential viewers and the unlikelihood that the graffiti will be painted over. These spots tend to be where young people from all over the city are likely to congregate, and thus the East Village, the Lower East Side, and SoHo are the places where most of the illegal New York City graffiti can be found. These are not poor, crime-ridden neighborhoods. To be sure, wealthier neighborhoods are more likely to have the resources to keep spots graffiti-free, and thus unattractive to writers (no one wants to spend the time and energy to do graffiti that will be painted over in twenty-four hours, because there's no fame). However, some poorer neighborhoods remain relatively graffiti-free because of their isolation, whereas wealthy neighborhoods that are attractive to young people and tourists tend to be riddled with graffiti.

Because graffiti writers want their names to be seen by the largest possible audience, they tend to write where there are higher concentrations of people. This does not mean that New York writers write exclusively in Manhattan; the city's best writers have their names up in high-traffic areas in every borough and are considered "all-city." But if you want to make a name for yourself as a graffiti writer, the quickest and easiest way to do that is to put your tag up in Manhattan, a lot. In the outer boroughs good spots are along major subway and traffic routes. Rooftops along the Brooklyn–Queens Expressway, and those that can be seen when the subway comes above ground—along the Number 7 subway line in Queens, and the 4/5 subway line in the Bronx—are prime locations for graffiti writers to paint their names.

Because space is at such a premium in Manhattan, graffiti murals occur almost exclusively in the outer boroughs, like Queens, the Bronx, and Brooklyn, that have more available wall space. This means that the graffiti in Manhattan is not the type that most people consider art; rather, Manhattan graffiti is mostly tags and throw-ups.

While "broken windows" rhetoric, tactics, and results have been criticized by criminologists, legal scholars, and sociologists, few have studied the direct relationship between graffiti and violent crime. And while politicians often suggest that graffiti vandals must be stopped before they become hardened criminals, rather than professional artists or scholars, few researchers have investigated the correlation (or lack thereof) between the amount of graffiti in a neighborhood and the amount of crime.

Graffiti thus presents a unique opportunity for studying "quality of life" crimes because, unlike alcohol drinking, weed smoking, or panhandling, there is undisputable visual evidence that it has occurred. We can photograph the graffiti in a specific area and compare that to the amount of crime that occurs in that space.

If we look at the map that indicates the amount of violent crime in specific neighborhoods in the city, the "broken windows" theory would predict that the highest concentrations of graffiti would occur in those areas with the highest crime rates, and that areas with low rates of violent crime, like downtown Manhattan, should be relatively graffiti free. However, nearly the opposite is true.

To make this point I will compare the crime statistics from two New York City police precincts: the First Precinct in Manhattan, which includes neighborhoods like SoHo and Tribeca, and the Seventy-first Precinct in Brooklyn, which includes my own neighborhood of Prospect Heights.

In 2006 in SoHo there were 0 murders, 3 rapes, 18 robberies, 17 acts of felonious assault, and 57 acts of burglary. In Prospect Heights, there

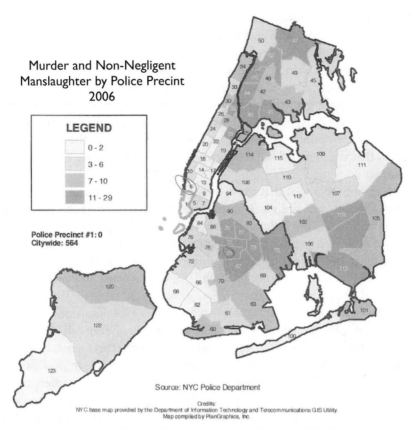

Murder and Non-Negligent Manslaughter by Police Precinct, 2006,
New York City Police Department.

were 3 murders, 3 rapes, 59 robberies, 66 acts of felonious assault, and
50 acts of burglary. Clearly with respect to violent crime, the Seventy-first
Precinct is a more dangerous neighborhood than the First Precinct. When
we compare the photographs of graffiti from the two neighborhoods, however, "broken windows" advocates would incorrectly predict that SoHo is
the higher crime area, because it has more graffiti.

Neighborhoods have different physical characteristics, making it difficult to compare the amount of graffiti in an exact quantitative fashion.
However, I begin this analysis by comparing something that exists in every
neighborhood of the city and is popular with graffiti writers, namely, mailboxes. Because they are under the purview of the federal government, we
can assume that the impetus to keep the mailboxes graffiti-free is roughly

the same throughout the city. In 2007 in Prospect Heights I photographed every mailbox on Franklin, Classon, Washington, and Vanderbilt avenues, from Eastern Parkway to Atlantic Avenue. In SoHo I photographed every mailbox on Prince, Spring, and Broome streets from Broadway to West Broadway. The photos show that while the Brooklyn mailboxes are not completely graffiti-free, the SoHo mailboxes are covered with graffiti tags. If we move from mailboxes to doors and walls, the same is true. The Brooklyn photos show a fair amount of graffiti, but the SoHo photos show that the neighborhood is covered with tags on nearly every available surface.

The photographs that show the heavily written walls and doors come from the safe and posh neighborhood of SoHo, whereas the photos that show comparatively little graffiti come from the neighborhood with over 30 percent more reported violent crime. Clearly the relationship between vandalism and violent crime is not nearly as causal as we are made to believe. High concentrations of graffiti vandalism exist in neighborhoods with little or no violent crime.

From these photos it is clear that SoHo has a "graffiti problem," yet we barely hear media reports about this, nor are there ever calls to clean up SoHo graffiti. SoHo has a reputation as a former artists' enclave, and for many tourists and shoppers this is part of the attraction. In on-line shopping guides SoHo is described as "trendy," with "charming" streets and adventurous restaurants, and as one of New York's "hottest" neighborhoods where celebrities are often seen shopping at high-end boutiques like Marc Jacobs, Betsey Johnson, Kate Spade, Coach, and Chanel.

To be sure, part of the attitude that SoHo residents and business owners have toward graffiti is explained by the connections between SoHo graffiti and some of its most famous artists. In the 1980s artists transformed SoHo's abandoned factory spaces into giant loft studios that made the neighborhood the center of art in the city. This is the area where Keith Haring and Jean-Michel Basquiat transitioned away from street art and became sought-after professional studio artists. The energy of those times and the graffiti subculture that these artists were loosely affiliated with still exists today and is showcased on the walls and doors of SoHo. And some creative entrepreneurs even attempt to mimic a sort of graffiti style to provide tourists with gritty souvenirs of the "real" New York City.

Despite all of the negativity associated with graffiti, it remains one of SoHo's selling points, literally. As these photos show, residents, tourists, and high-end boutiques co-exist with graffiti vandalism in a relatively symbiotic fashion. Further, SoHo attracts the type of urban "cool" consumer that marketers call "taste makers" and that advertisers and retailers so desperately want to reach.

The clothing store Yellow Rat Bastard at 480 Broadway in the center of SoHo is case in point. This store sells skateboards, sneakers, and hip hop fashions to a sophisticated and savvy urban clientele, and they allow and even encourage graffiti writers to tag the interior of their store. The graffiti on these walls is supposed to tell shoppers that this is a cool space, and the gear that they buy signals to themselves and others that they, too, are cool. Incidentally, real New York City writers see this act of co-optation for what it is, a way of using graffiti to sell products, and hence you see very few famous writers on the walls. But still, the vandalism is good for business.

For the "sneakerheads"—that is, the kids who collect rare sneakers, which are often sold and re-sold on eBay for thousands of dollars—the graffiti on the walls surrounding the store are as important as the sneakers on sale inside. For the past decade graffiti artists such as COPE, ESPO, STASH, DES, NECK FACE, and CLAW have all designed limited-edition sneakers for corporations like Nike, Puma, Adidas, and Vans. For the kids who wait in line, sometimes for days, for an opportunity to purchase these products, the tags on the surrounding walls by well-known graffiti artists signals that they are in the right place, and further illustrates the graffiti consumption nexus. Graffiti writers' status as illegal outlaw artists makes the product even more desirable. If the purchaser can also recognize the artists' illegal work on the streets surrounding the store, the status of the wearer, as a transgressive outsider, is further enhanced. Graffiti writing in SoHo therefore appears not to be the menace that police and politicians insist it is, and in some cases even offers an experience that provides consumers with symbolic confirmation of their own transgressive identities.

Collage of Brooklyn mailboxes.

Collage of SoHo mailboxes.

Collage of SoHo graffiti.

GETTING 2 UP

VERT

First Contact

On a rainy November afternoon in midtown Manhattan, Tim walked up to me at the Donnell Library, took off his headphones, and shook my hand. In that handshake I felt a confidence that I hadn't yet known, and when our eyes met I saw my friend in a whole new light. The person I knew before as Tim had changed into VERT, the graffiti writer. In that moment I also changed, from a man whose identity as a graduate student was grounded in independence and knowledge to an ignorant neophyte stepping into a strange, new world. We were there for a screening of the film *Style Wars*, which at that time was unavailable on video or DVD.

VERT is twenty-two, five-foot-eight with an athletic build. He has Irish-looking features with brown hair and his skin has a reddish tint. He wears wire-framed glasses but doesn't look bookish, and he has a booming smile. His fashion sense is another matter; some might call him sloppy, but non-assuming, practical, or even punk would be a better way to put it.

VERT is the second-oldest of three boys and he grew up in Norwalk, Connecticut. Tim, like a lot of Irish Catholics, myself included, has had experience with alcoholism in his family, and although VERT doesn't have a problem with alcohol, I think that he would consider himself a recovering graffiti addict. Tim was a suburban introvert who became obsessed with the culture and music of New York City, and through his secret life as a graffiti writer he created his own cache of urban cool. VERT started graffiti at around fourteen, when a local Norwalk friend handed him a pen and told him to hurry and think up a tag. Tim took the pen and wrote "FADE" on the wall. He would eventually settle on VERT, a skateboard term that, as horizontal's opposite, also had sexual connotations in his clique. In the early 1990s he hooked up with Connecticut legends CROMAG (R.I.P.) and EROC and started coming into the city to bomb (paint illegally) and attend shows of hardcore bands.[1]

Graffiti culture is made up of an eclectic population that traverses racial, ethnic, and class lines, a fact that is often reflected in the tastes and styles of the writers.[2] VERT's participation in graffiti is an example of how graffiti is a bridge between various subcultures. He is one of many graffiti kids who can skateboard, mosh, and break dance.[3] He has seen the hardcore group the Cro-Mags and hip hop legend KRS-ONE, and knows the lyrics to both. For VERT, graffiti is what he does and punk, hardcore, and rap are the music that he listens to.

Beef

Beef—disputes between writers that arise from intense competition—is a big part of the culture of graffiti and the issue that interests idealistic researchers the least. Beef results in crossing out other writers' names, going over pieces, lots of stories about violence, and sometimes actual violence. I am five-foot-ten, 170 pounds, and not much of a fighter. Some researchers who have studied violent gang cultures, like Martin Jankowski, know martial arts and could handle themselves. I do not share this distinction.[4] This, for me, is the most difficult part of studying graffiti. There's always this uncomfortable feeling that one slip-up or misspoken word could lead to a physical confrontation. This scares me. Fortunately, most of the writers I have met have been extremely cool, but you don't always know who has beef with whom, and I was always wary of unintentionally offending someone, and taking on the consequences of someone else's beef simply by being associated with him or her.

VERT likes to *talk* about beef and insists that it is a significant part of the culture. Some lesser-known writers will initiate beef with more established writers to get noticed. This is a treacherous act and can come to physical confrontation if the beef is not "squashed" (i.e., a truce is not called). However, for many, the creation of beef is also a catalyst to their creativity. For others beef is a sign that they're starting to have an impact on the culture, gaining recognition from kings who rule through grace and force.

Graffiti is violent and competitive. Even when writers are careful and respect others' work, beef is nearly inescapable. There are many reasons to have beef, including territorial and stylistic transgressions, but adolescent machismo also plays a large part.[5] Lots of graffiti writers like to fight, and it is this aspect of the culture that is most exciting to them. The drama tends to curtail as writers get older, but not always; many writers channel their energy into the study of martial arts and boxing and continue to engage in sanctioned and unsanctioned bouts.

VERT, illustration of the page for "Sexy" from the author's blackbook.

VERT told me that the current level of violence in the subculture pales in comparison to what it was in the 1980s, but beef continues to be a defining aspect.[6] Unwillingness to fight, either for yourself or for your friends or members of your crew, will result in a brief writing career. This violent aspect of graffiti also explains why fewer women are attracted to the culture, although many excellent female writers have been successful in this environment.

While actual fighting is part of graffiti culture, much of this drama takes place on the walls. These walls are the site of a whole new set of stories where each word has a history and a meaning. These dramas are for the most part not actual; they occur in virtual time and space. It is likely that you will never meet the person you have a beef with face to face. As VERT says, "It's weird when graffiti writers meet because you never know whether or not you have beef with this person."

VERT took me to a tiny smoke shop on West Broadway between Canal and Grand that doubles as a graffiti supply store. Inside Soho Down and Under, as it was called then, I was overwhelmed at how vast this graffiti universe is, and how little I knew.[7] There were magazines, videos, t-shirts, and spray nozzles called "caps." I wanted them all, but they were not cheap. Eventually I chose the magazines *On the Go* #10 and *Stress* #1 and the video *Video Graff* #9.[8]

We left the store and continued walking in the rain on our mini-tour of SoHo's graffiti. I had been in SoHo many times, but now I was seeing it as if for the first time. VERT told me that SoHo's history as the center of New York City art has made it a graffiti tourist spot. He pointed out that tags from writers all over the country and the world can be found there.

VERT interpreted some of the work for me, including a fresh orange and red GOLD that had a bulldog for an "O" (GOLD is an alias for graffiti legend ZEPHYR). It can be difficult for the untrained eye to read graffiti, much of which is done in complicated "wildstyle," but writers can fairly easily make out and read most graffiti. These pieces seemed quite new. VERT told me that these were "legal walls" and the writers had gotten permission from property owners to paint.

Catching a Tag

In preparation for my meeting with VERT I had spontaneously bought a marker and practiced tagging on a big stack of scrap paper at home. My tags were terrible. I wrote G-ES, a pun on the word guess and my initials, G.S., which I thought was pretty clever. I left the house with my marker in my jacket pocket. As I traveled to midtown I was full of ideas of great places to hit. All self-expression makes you feel vulnerable in some way, and I was nervous about putting my mark on something in such a public way. However, I could not stifle the desire to experience just a bit of what this felt like. I had to participate in the culture in an effort to understand what it is that writers do—and because, quite frankly, it looked like fun.

VERT and I headed north on West Broadway, and as we walked through a covered sidewalk that had blue plywood walls with no tags on them, I mustered my courage and said, "Wanna tag it?" I pulled my fat red Pilot marker out of my coat and wrote my alias, quick and ugly, remembering to put a halo over it like I had seen VERT do in the pages of my journal to try and give some semblance of graffiti style.[9] Nevertheless, my tag was awful and I was embarrassed. I passed the marker to VERT and he said, "Keep a lookout." This jolted me into awareness that, while I had been worried about writing something silly and about posing as a member of a subculture I wasn't involved in, the fact that this was illegal had not concerned me.[10] I knew that I did not want to get caught, but the chances of that seemed slight because I had deliberately chosen a spot away from foot traffic. I marveled at VERT's tag, which he executed with effortless panache. He also tagged his crew, "CST," under it. Typically, crews are three-letter acronyms that have multiple meanings. CST stands for "can't stop tagging" and "community service team," among other things.

Today's writers have a more intimate relationship with the entire city. In the 1970s and 1980s graffiti was location-specific and was mainly written on trains. Nowadays you need to know where to look to find the best graffiti, and being part of the culture means that you know the spots. When I asked VERT how graffiti has changed, he said that he thinks that it has become more subtle. Most people no longer see graffiti as a mainstream issue, which is why politicians and police have to remind us that it is still a problem. Present-day graffiti is an esoteric phenomenon appealing to those who are in the know and know what to look for.

I thanked VERT for bringing me up to speed and raced home, eager to read my new magazines. The scope of the information that I was gathering was staggering. I had been under the impression that graffiti writers would welcome me into their circle because I had recognized that they were doing something with deep intellectual and artistic significance. In talking to VERT and looking at the photos and articles in the magazines, however, I felt like an intruder. That night before going to bed I made a commitment to come up with a research strategy that would involve writers in the articulation of their culture. I needed something that would encourage writers to show a different side of themselves and hopefully form a bridge between us. That strategy wound up being the blackbook, in which I would give writers opportunities to illustrate words for the purpose of fomenting a dialogue.

WRITER'S BLOCK

Blackbook in the Streets

$\mathcal{S}$oho Down and Under is a small store owned by a Lebanese man who has been in New York City since 1975. He has been at the current location on West Broadway and Canal Street for the past three years. Before that, he and his brother owned the deli across the street, which the older writers called Soho Zat. Carl Westin and the guys from Videograf, who make underground videos of writers doing graffiti, had their clandestine offices in the same building and gave the deli owners their tapes to sell.[1] Word got out and the tapes sold well, and soon the shop started selling other graffiti-related items like *International Graffiti Times*, the first graffiti magazine. When they lost the lease at the deli, they opened the current smaller shop and continued selling graffiti products.

The owner of this Bohemian business[2] wears his knit cap with the logo slightly to the side. His card, which was obviously done by a writer, has the slogan "All Your Graff Needs & More." In addition to magazines, t-shirts, books, and videos, Soho Down and Under sells different kinds of "caps" that fit on aerosol cans and are used to vary the width of spray paint. Today they also sell the paint brands Molotow and Montana, which are specifically designed by writers for graffiti art.

As I was locking up my bicycle outside the store the day after my excursion with VERT, I could sense that the young writers hanging out in front viewed me with a degree of skepticism. I heard mumbled phrases about the vandal squad and the police as I was being sized up by the collective of about seven writers. Finally, one of the writers asked me the question that I had been preparing for: "You a writer?"

"No," I replied, "I'm a researcher and I'm writing a book on graffiti." Suddenly, the safe distance that these kids had placed between themselves and me disappeared and I was surrounded by enthusiastic young people. I introduced myself and asked each of them what name they wrote. Next, I

CLIF, illustration of the page for "Art" from the author's blackbook.

described my project to them and showed them the blackbook I had created the night before,[3] which was filled with words to be pieced (drawn). I made my initial request to CLIF, who was the first writer to introduce himself.

I told CLIF that he could do any word he wanted and passed him the book. The rest of us continued to talk as CLIF paged through the book looking at the words. He came across one he liked and announced it proudly to the assembled crew: "I'm doing 'art.'" There was a slight hush as CLIF took out his Pilot Precise Rolling Ball pen and began to draw. Then the talk resumed around him.

CLIF, an eighteen-year-old Haitian immigrant who lives with his family in Brooklyn, has a constant smile on his face and speaks with a bit of a Creole accent. He was wearing a dark blue Ralph Lauren Polo Sport cap, a green and black Columbia Jacket, black jeans and boots. CLIF continued to talk while he pieced. I glanced at what he had done so far—drawing what appeared to be a clown.

Two kids standing next to CLIF were checking out the copy of the book *Subway Art* that I had given them to look at. I was surprised that they didn't know the history of their own subculture, but it was nice to hear them "ooh," "aah," and "OHHH shit!" as they mined the pages of the old masters. Both of these writers were Dominicans from the Bronx. There was another writer just outside of this group who was close enough to hear us, but was not part of the conversation. He was curious about me, and we kept making eye contact. More and more kids came over to check out CLIF's piece and that loosened our initial circle. Writers began to filter in and out, and CLIF started talking with the writer who had been on the outside of the circle looking in. He had on a black DKNY hat, black North Face jacket, blue jeans, and Timberland boots. He had little dreads poking out from under his cap, and his skin was dark and clear. He looked African-American though he told me later that one of his parents was from Panama.

As CLIF was piecing, I tried to offer him some markers to use but he declined when he saw that I had brought cheap ninety-eight-cent Paper Mate markers. Even though it wasn't that cold out, CLIF kept complaining that his hands were getting too cold to piece, so he suggested we go around the corner to the sandwich shop on Canal Street to finish up.

CLIF led the writer with the black North Face jacket and myself around the corner to get warm. They sat down at a table while I waited in line to get some coffee. When I rejoined them I offered my hand to the new kid as we had yet to formally meet. He introduced himself as TESAA. I sat down across from CLIF and watched him piece while TESAA and I talked. TESAA and CLIF also talked to each other. They had just met and appeared to be getting along nicely. We discussed different writers we were familiar with, and then CLIF offered *his* blackbook for me to check out. It was incredible, and I wondered if someday the book CLIF was holding would

TA, throw-up illustration from the author's blackbook.

ever compare to the one he had just handed me. There was so much energy on those pages and CLIF had a story for each one. The blackbook, or piece book, also acts like an autograph book for writers, and CLIF's was filled with some of New York's most famous writers, including COPE and JA, which he made it a point to show me.

CLIF was about finished with his piece, so I started testing my theory on TESAA. I explained to him that I thought that graffiti creates its own symbolic language, and that by piecing words that have a constructed mainstream meaning, graffiti writers enter into a discussion with the larger population about the symbolic power of language. TESAA responded, "Yeah, modern hieroglyphics, we create its meaning." I wasn't sure what he meant but I liked it.

CLIF finished his piece. He had opened the book and written on both pages, and along with his clown face he added the word "art" three times and "CLIF" twice. He also made a plea to other writers: "Let's preserve art, not destroy it." He also urged the cops to "leave graffiti artists alone." I took the book and showed it to TESAA, who seemed impressed. I asked TESAA if he wanted to do a word but he declined, saying he was too tired to do a good job. I asked him to tag one of the blank pages in the back and he started doing a green throw-up of "TA."

While TESAA was drawing, his enthusiasm for graff was bubbling over. He talked about when he was little and he used to sit in the window of his apartment and watch the trains go by. "I was mesmerized," he said.

"What? You were like four or five years old?"

TESAA said, "Yeah, I just loved it. I love graff, I ain't never gonna quit graff. I'm gonna be like forty and still painting. It's like a drug." He gave the book back, and he had written "Modern Hiero" next to his fill-in. I thought it was a play on "hero" but TESAA laughed at me and said, "No, Modern Hieroglyphics."[4]

We left the sandwich shop and continued our discussion outside of Soho Down and Under, where the formerly assembled writers' convention had dissipated. We talked about the legal risks involved in writing graffiti. Writers pass stories around like germs, and TESAA said he heard that in Los Angeles the police do graffiti entrapment; the cops supposedly will paint a wall in an effort to entice writers to paint on it, and when they do the cops will jump out from their hiding spots and bust them.

We left each other around 5:15. CLIF said he'd call me the next time he did a "legal wall." This was only the second time I had heard that term, but I assumed it meant somehow getting permission to paint legally.

Two weeks later CLIF called from a pay phone. He told me a story about a piece that he had just finished on Avenue D on the Lower East Side. When I tried to get him to tell me the cross street he said he didn't know. He said that he roamed all over trying to find someone who would give him permission to paint. CLIF doesn't paint illegally because he wants to avoid trouble with the law, yet this doesn't discourage him. He said, "If you have a talent for something you got to find ways to express it." CLIF told me that he paid the owner of a Chinese restaurant fifty dollars to paint his wall. He said he didn't have a phone and that he'd call again. That was the last I heard from him, and I never saw his name "up" in the streets. He turned out to be what writers call a "toy," a neophyte who talks a big game but leaves the culture as quickly as he or she enters it. I went searching for the piece he did but never found it.[5] Instead, a door on First Avenue and Twelfth Street captured my attention.

Reading Graffiti

There is narrative to a wall that goes beyond individual tags claiming space. Numerous tags on a wall provide writers with the opportunity to tell stories about the exploits of their peers. A wall with tags and throw-ups on it will stimulate a writer to narrate a scenario; not only who was here, but who was here first, who has beef with whom, who's more talented, who's in from out of town, who's in from different boroughs, whose tags are getting better, and whose are getting worse.

Door covered in graffiti, 1st Ave, East Village, 1996.

Although tags can be visually interesting on their own,[6] a single tag does not provide this impetus to the imagination. Rather, it is how the different tags play off of one another that reveals the creative energy of a wall. There is an organic order to the way the space is divided, and a wall or door with heavy layers of graffiti reveals a history to its viewers in the same way that the sedimentary layers of ancient ruins inspire archaeologists to tell tales of past civilizations.[7]

In the spring of 1996 there was a door on First Avenue that had about twelve tags on it. I will describe three that I came to know because they were easy to read. I have never personally met TWIST, DRANE, or UFO, so my analysis is gleaned from conversations with writers and my reading of the walls and magazines. TWIST is a nationwide star. He has done gallery shows in San Francisco, New York, and Brazil, bombed D.C. buses, tagged New York City mailboxes relentlessly. The writer AME told me that TWIST "bombed the Great Wall of China; I haven't seen the flicks but it's bona fide." TWIST's tag is thick and is done with a homemade marker called a "mop" filled with industrial-grade Marsh ink. It is the largest on the door, which shows that he is a confident writer. One writer I spoke with, KEST, guessed that other people were up on the door prior to TWIST, but no one else wrote on the bottom half of the door because it is awkward to bend over and write, but that "TWIST finds a way to make weird spaces work for him."

DRANE also has a back story that I've picked up through reading his tags and talking to other writers. DRANE is up all over the East Village, but I hear he is from Ohio. DRANE's style is easy to read, and thus I am able to recognize it all over downtown New York. For many of his tags, DRANE also uses a mop to get a broad black ink stroke similar to TWIST.

The third writer under scrutiny I will call the "UFO bomber" because he doesn't have a name. This writer has completely broken free from letters and style. He (or she) tags up an ugly looking spaceship that I've seen everywhere in Williamsburg and Manhattan. The frequency of this writer's work near more established writers suggests that he believes that the originality of his spaceship is on par with the stylized writers. The drips look forced, sometimes he puts an eye in the middle and writes "UFO" or "907 CREW" next to it.

The UFO bomber is a fairly recent phenomenon, so I assume that he was the last writer to tag the door. From this it follows that UFO is not intimidated by more established artists. We can now tell numerous stories just by looking at this wall. TWIST's tag is big, taking up a large section of the door and leaving only a small amount of space for other writers to get up. DRANE put his name in the awkward space that TWIST had left open. DRANE was careful not to "go over" TWIST's tag, showing his respect for TWIST as well as announcing his own skills for accepting TWIST's indirect challenge of putting his tag in a difficult spot. It takes skill to make your mark in this way, and therefore we can assume that DRANE is a pretty good writer. How do we assess what UFO is trying to say? Is this to be construed as a major challenge to these writers' notions of style, or is it just a toy on a wall?[8]

The narrative possibilities that this door holds are almost endless, and further it matters little if my postulations are correct. Utilizing your imagination for storytelling is a creative act inspired by what many consider to be just ugly markings with no meaning behind them. The story I have just told only looked at three of the twelve tags on the beige door, but for ten minutes I was completely consumed and forgot that I was standing on a busy street in Manhattan.

Graffiti writing incites stories, and the desire to write graffiti in part comes from the need to be part of the story. In the introduction to *The Art of Getting Over: Graffiti at the Millennium*, Steve Powers writes, "Stories are the most permanent medium for storing and sharing the graffiti experience. . . . Good stories go across the world in minutes and last forever."

Stories are an essential part of city life, and the way that graffiti animates space is an enjoyable, fascinating aspect of the urban experience. French architecture critic Michel de Certeau agrees with this notion, arguing that graffiti is in line with a collection of urban activities in which we make our own stories and produce the memories that make space habitable. This lived space is the space of everyday experience, in contrast to the planned, ordered city that seeks to impose a metanarrative on space. This may be more than just enjoyment; the author of the renowned Marxist text *The Production of Space*, Henri Lefebvre, believes that transforming space in this fashion is potentially radical, and that the reevaluation of space is as critical to social change as economic and political restructuring.[9]

Welcome to ESPO Land

On Bedford and South Fifth, near the Williamsburg Bridge in Brooklyn, I discovered a small refrigeration shop covered with the large colorful murals that writers call pieces. Crowning the top of the building is an orange billboard that appears to be an advertisement done in the style of the old "Greetings from Asbury Park" ads, in which the letters contained scenic representations of tourist attractions. I whipped out my camera and started photographing the colorful pieces that laced the bottom of the building. After weeks of riding my bike over the bridge, I took a closer look at the billboard. It said "Greetings From ESPOLAND where the Quality of Life is Offensive." Inside each letter was an iconographic representation of all of quality of life crimes, from purse-snatching to low-level marijuana sales. VERT had told me about a writer named ESPO, and it finally hit me. Holy shit, I thought, that's graffiti too? In one instant my perception of what graffiti was and what it could be was blown wide open. I was giddy with delight. ESPO had found a loophole. ESPO knows that if he conforms to the accepted aesthetic standards of advertising his work will not be viewed as illegal and he can paint in broad daylight. The artistic skill it takes to produce graffiti that looks like advertising is impressive, but ESPO is taking a big risk courting mainstream audiences who might be more dismissive of traditional-looking graffiti. More importantly, he also has a message about perception that plays on our preconceptions. He knows that his iconic rendering will actually deflect attention. ESPO put what the mainstream supposedly hates, illegal graffiti, right under our noses and few noticed.

ESPO was utilizing mainstream ideas about what advertising and graffiti are supposed to look like in order to comment on how we fail to see. The joke was on me, until I accepted ESPO's challenge of seeing things differently. He shows an appreciation for the letter style and graphic design

73

ESPOLand, Williamsburg, Brooklyn, circa 1996 (detail).

of these classic sign painters, and thus places graffiti writing directly in that tradition of urban painters.[1] In fact, ESPO is so confident that those who do notice something interesting are going to appreciate his work that he leaves his phone number. On the bottom of the piece it reads, "For tour info call: (212) 592-0903."

I raced home and called the number. The greeting informed me that I'd reached *On the Go* magazine, of which ESPO is the editor and publisher. I left a message for ESPO praising his billboard piece and some of the articles he'd written, and then explained how I was using a blackbook to do research on graffiti.

A few days later ESPO returned my call. He seemed intrigued by my idea. We talked about graffiti, and I got the impression that he was feeling me out. We spoke of the books and articles that had thus far provided most of my knowledge about the culture. At this stage in my education,

Getting Up by Craig Castleman was my bible, but when I brought it up ESPO praised the book but also said that it painted too rosy a picture of graffiti culture. According to ESPO, Castleman failed to capture the importance of beef—the violence that graffiti writers commit toward each other. ESPO's continued discussion of the more grisly side of writing culture made a deep impression on me.

We continued our phone relationship for about two months, and then one day ESPO invited me to a spot where a friend of his was showing some photographs. This was to be the first time we met in person. He gave me the address to McGovern's Bar at 300 Spring Street and told me he'd be there around 7:00.

I took a seat at a table facing the door and waited for ESPO to arrive. Finally ESPO entered the dark bar. He was a fairly big white dude with angular features and close-cropped, dark brown hair. He was wearing a green and maroon Columbia ski jacket, khaki pants (not too baggy), and new, low-top, black canvas Nike Air Force One sneakers with a yellow stripe—not exactly the hip hop uniform that I expected from the editor of *On the Go*.[2]

I got up to greet ESPO, a little nervous to meet the man who was rapidly becoming one of my heroes. He sat down across from me and I gave him a copy of a chapter that I had just completed. Then I showed him some pictures I had taken. Feeling like I was talking to a celebrity, I gushed praise. ESPO was very humble and just gave me a nod for going out and taking photos of graffiti. As ESPO and I talked, he glanced at the flicks and then slid them to his friend Ed, a blond white guy with thinning hair and a goatee, who started to go through them. Within seconds Ed interrupted and said, "That's my work right there," pointing to a purple piece in the lower left-hand corner of the photo of the refrigeration shop. "Really?" I said, grasping my research opportunity. "What do you write?"

When he told me, my body tensed with fear. The only other writer I knew at the time had beef with this guy. I pushed my blackbook across the table to ESPO, trying not to show my nerves. Then Ed spoke up: "Whatever you do, don't put this kid in your book. This kid's a herb," he chided as he showed me a picture of a piece done by the other graffiti writer I knew. I was silent and embarrassed. I made no effort to defend my friend. I rationalized that I needed to make more contacts, but still it didn't seem quite right. The writer then picked up the blackbook and began to page through it while I explained the concept to him, not knowing how my affiliation to other writers would be viewed. I remained calm on the outside but desperately hoped that this would not lead to a confrontation. The moment came when he saw the other writer's piece, but he was cool and just turned the page.[3]

I sighed with relief and returned my attention to ESPO, wondering if he knew what I had just gone through. If he did, he didn't let on and passed me a leather-bound portfolio filled with pictures of pieces that he had done along with newspaper clippings on some of his work. Our table was now surrounded by writers, who were all introducing themselves to me and trying to see what the blackbook was all about. HUSH held center stage, paging through the book and offering critical commentary on the words I had chosen. He was trying to decide what word to do, but DASH grabbed the book and started checking it out with his friend CRO. CRO took the black Sharpie I offered and started to piece fiendishly at the table behind me.

I continued to get ESPO's story. I learned that we were both born in 1968. He is from Philadelphia and went to college there at the University of the Arts. He studied graphic design because they gave him financial aid, but he considers himself a painter. He has been living in New York since 1994. Even though he is the publisher and editor of a magazine, he says that he isn't very good at graphic design; on paper he likes to use words to express himself. He started writing graffiti at a relatively late age, but in the past ten years his ethos hasn't changed much.

When I first started writing I was already old. I was going on seventeen when I started. My Mom was a strong moral guide, but she didn't really give a shit either way about graffiti. But my sisters, oh man, they let me know. They saw every trick I did and they were like "Yo, don't do that shit." Even my friends who did graff in eighth and ninth grade by the time they were juniors in high school when I started, they were like, "What the fuck is that, you really wanna do that shit? That shit is kinda corny." So my remedy for that situation was to go out to a different spot every week and do a piece. Three or four colors, ten colors if I could pull it off, blow up the spot and make it look nice. Every week it was like a rooftop, or it was some down-low spot that I heard about. I was going out and just painting different spots around the city, and it was getting to a point that other writers could set their clocks by it. Okay, it's Friday night, ES-PO's doing something somewhere. I had a rep for that, and that was my shit. Finally dudes were like, you're not really bombing, Philly is all about bombing. So I'd go out and saturate a couple bus routes with tags, but it wasn't my main thing. My main thing was painting and getting the flick and showing my boys and getting feedback. The first fifteen to twenty weeks I went out my stuff sucked, and it was a very horrible process. But I learned and I just kept going back for more, and I just enjoyed it so much. And it kept me out of drinking and driving, and it kept me out of so many of the typical drug- and alcohol-related dramas that my friends were going through. And to this day it's still about that for me.

Some more kids came over to greet ESPO, and I took the opportunity to check up on CRO and DASH. CRO was an amiable twenty-seven-year-old Puerto Rican from Queens. He had chosen the word "wreck" in my black-book and was piecing with a black Sharpie Fine Point Permanent Marker. I included "wreck" because I thought it would give writers an opportunity to comment on the perception that all graffiti is destructive. CRO's style was complicated but readable. The letters were interconnected, with each letter forming an integral part of the next.

I asked him why he chose "wreck." "I don't know", he said. "I just like the letters." I was all set to ask him about vandalism, but he just kept talking about letters and I couldn't get a word in. He told me that being able to get creative with letters that aren't in your name is a sign of a writer's skills. "I know writers who only practice their names and I'm like, 'Yo, I'll piece your name and you piece mine.' A lot of writers won't do it." As he was finishing up, he started asking me questions about why I put the black-book together. When I told him I was curious about the culture's power to give words new meanings, he was polite but then he cut me off and told me that he thought the blackbook worked on a more basic level. CRO explained that my book forces writers to explore other letters, something that they might not normally do. As writers grow they move from mastery of their name to mastery of the alphabet, and in doing so they discover that some letters work well together and some don't. I try to clarify this for myself. "Do you mean that you pieced 'wreck' because of how the letters look rather than what the word means?"

"Exactly."

CRO, illustration of the page for "Wreck" from the author's blackbook.

Similar to most graduate students in 1996, I was obsessed with discourse and constructed meaning. I was desperately searching for discursive strategies that would empower those who had been labeled outsiders to redefine language in their own terms. All of these issues seemed somehow less important to me as I stared at the word on the page. W-R-E-C-K. Angle, curve, straight, curve, angle. Wow, what a beautifully symmetric word. The E seems to center it and becomes the focus of my attention. Then I notice the similarity between the R and the C, and finally I move out to the W and the K. The letters in this word fit perfectly. I am no longer concerned with the meaning of this word, and I wonder how many other words display this elegance. I then realize that a writer chooses his graffiti name based on the shape and connections of a word, as well as what the word means. To disregard meaning altogether in order to focus on the aesthetics of the letters was a whole new way to look at language and the process of writing graffiti. The blackbook, which allowed writers to perform in a specific context, forced me to expand my theory of what I thought graffiti culture was and to concentrate just as closely on the lessons that the writers themselves could teach.

By 11:00 I'd known ESPO for two hours, but it seemed like longer. We were seated on barstools with our backs to the bar. "How's it going?" he said, referring to the success of my meetings with various writers, which he seemed proud to have instigated. I asked ESPO if he was going to piece my book and he said, "Someday when you can part with the book I'd like to take it for a few days so I can do it right." I had no idea that this was common practice, and I gave it to him thinking it was a huge gesture of trust.

Return Trip

Over a week later I met ESPO at McGovern's to retrieve the blackbook. I found to my satisfaction that he had done quite a few pages. When ESPO took possession of the blackbook five words had been completed; after he returned it, thirteen words had been pieced. He had the book for over a week and he found time to put his mark on "style," "struggle," "bomb," "rhythm," "authority," "fresh," "fame," and "vandal." He also passed the book along to his friends MEEZ (from Philly) and NAVEL, who took the opportunity to do throw-ups on the blank pages.

ESPO's premiere piece is "struggle," in which he used layers of post office stickers to give the piece texture. He also used the stickers to create a space larger than the page, like a magazine fold-out advertisement. The technical sophistication of this piece shows clearly that "struggle" was a labor of love. Then ESPO took a picture out of his pocket of the Unabomber piece that he had painted in the Amtrak tunnel that runs from 72nd to 125th under Riverside Drive. I thought that he was giving me the picture and I opened my photo album. ESPO said, "Unfortunately, this is my only copy."

"Then I'll have to go myself," I resolved.

ESPO, "Unabomber" piece, Freedom Tunnel, 1996.

ESPO

Illustrating "Struggle"

ᴇSPO's "struggle" piece, like most of his work, goes beyond the parameters of the page. ᴇSPO's sticker technique also means that he will have the biggest piece, which in the competitive culture of graffiti, means better. I am extremely excited that this experiment in visual sociology is working. I chose "struggle" because I was interested in political activism and empowerment, and even though I pressed ᴇSPO on these issues it was clear that his definition of politics is different from mine. This suggests once again that allowing informants a space to have a voice protects against imposing a theoretical frame around a culture, and ensures what ethnographers and others call grounded theory— theory that evolves out of field research, rather than sociological literature.

The piece itself is red, blue, and green with a yellow background called "3-D." The focal point of the piece is centered on the two G's. ᴇSPO has reversed the second G, to give the impression that the letters themselves are engaged in a struggle. The two G's each have arms and appear to be in an arm wrestling contest. Stars and exclamation points float above, reminiscent of the Boom! Pow! of comic books.

I interviewed ᴇSPO about the piece.

ᴇSPO, illustration of the page for "Struggle" from the author's blackbook.

GS: Why did you choose to piece "struggle"?

ESPO: Struggle is inherent to my style. There is no style in the easy route. In order to better your style you have to consistently raise the stakes with yourself.

GS: Would you have pieced "art" if it hadn't already been done?

ESPO: Nope.

GS: Did you originally plan to go off the page, or did that just come about in the course of the struggle?

ESPO: I started with the G's in a rush of inspiration. The problem of resolving the lack of space forced me to make the decision to use the stickers to make the page bigger.

GS: If you look on the back you can tell that first you did the G's in marker and then stickered over it. Is this how you were able to perfect your piece without erasing, something you can't do on a wall?

ESPO: I was applying the option that exists in painting, to go over and over an area until you get it right. I used the stickers to apply this concept to the confines of a blackbook.

GS: I like how technically sophisticated your "struggle" piece is. You use intricately cut and torn stickers and White Out with extreme exactitude and precision. Your materials are everyday items, government handouts, which are available to everyone. However, you choose to utilize these items in the service of art. I think that there is a politics of aesthetics here, a comment on how we choose to make our world using what we have around us. What do you think about the political connotations of your "struggle"?

ESPO: The use of the stickers is a tribute to the writers that made use of them. It's akin to the way TWIST decorates his canvasses with the nametag sticker borders. Using the ordinary and accessible and turning it into something new is pure hip hop. Struggle is growth. Without it, we are as good as tree sloths.

GS: Its philosophical meaning yes, but how does it translate into politics?

ESPO: Politically, using government handouts to create menacing art is like biting the hand that feeds you, which is as fresh as it gets, artistically.

GS: You once read me a quote about the difference between a criminal and an outlaw. Do you remember it?

ESPO: "There is a crucial difference between the criminal and the out-law. The criminal is a perverse rebel who acts out against the law, a subnormal person who is unable to care enough about others to bear adult responsibilities. The outlaw is a supra-normal person who cares about others too much to accept the limitations on Eros that are imposed by normal life. Thus the outlaw's quest moves outside and beyond, not against, the law. While the rebel is merely rejecting the established, the outlaw is motivated by a quest for self-government. . . . not rooted in any undigested psychological need to rebel but in a passion for justice, dignity, and freedom. The transmoral conscience of the outlaw is the inner voice of a universal community struggling to be born." [Sam Keen, *The Passionate Life: Stages of Loving*]

GS: Do you think that your "struggle" looks political in any way?

ESPO: The politically aware person who writes effectively cannot dis-guise their style anymore than a clotheshorse can hide a lust for DKNY. I hope all the pieces I do have a raw political nerve in them, as that's me.

GS: We've discussed before that many of your pieces strike with a double-edged sword aimed both at writers and at a larger mainstream audience. How would you want those in the main-stream with no understanding of graffiti to see your piece?

ESPO: I can't care what they see in it, as long as they see it. Lay peo-ple are blind to graff, so anything I can do to shake them out of their sleep is great. A while back I made the decision to elevate the scope of the stuff I was doing, but it was important for me to bring the old audience with me, so that's why there's a dou-ble and triple edge to what I do. I got a lot of demographics to touch.

INTO THE TUNNEL

Under Manhattan

Most graffiti writers say they write for a very simple reason: it's fun. For some this is linked to the thrill of getting away with what criminologist Jack Katz calls a "sneaky crime."[1] However, aside from the fun of making illegal art and getting famous for it, graffiti writing is also essentially about urban exploration. From the beginning graffiti writers have ventured to the most precarious places to put their marks. From high atop bridges and buildings to deep underground in subway tunnels, writers are explorers.

In the early 1980s, FREEDOM discovered an Amtrak tunnel that stretches from 72nd Street to 125th Street under Riverside Drive on the Upper West Side of Manhattan and turned it into his personal studio. Photos of FREEDOM's pieces were published in the book *Spraycan Art* by Chalfant and Prigoff, and this turned the spot into a graffiti landmark.

Graffiti writers exist on the margins of society, and this subculture often converges with other marginalized groups. FREEDOM developed relationships with the homeless men and women in the tunnel and was one of the guides for Jennifer Toth, a young anthropologist researching this dark underworld. This tunnel became the source of inspiration for Toth's 1993 book *The Mole People*, which was accompanied by Margaret Morton's photographic study of the tunnel. Their main contact in this world is Bernard Isaacs, a longtime resident who has earned the title "The Lord of the Tunnel."[2] Terry Williams had also been doing research on Bernard and his community, and he shared his unpublished field notes with me.

On a cold Saturday afternoon in February VERT, his friend Sacha, and I climb through a hole in a fence near Riverside Park and stand between two sets of train tracks. To the right, the tracks run south to Penn Station, to the left they run north into the tunnel and darkness.

The only thing I hear is the crunch, crunch of my boots on the rocky floor beating in time to my racing heart. It is dark, and I am scared. The cold February rain that trickles through the grates and lands on my neck reminds me of the world above, but as we continued further into the darkness the silence commands my consciousness and the tunnel's power begins to take effect.

VERT is a seasoned underground explorer, and I am following blindly as he walks confidently in the middle of the tracks. "How do you know if a train is coming?" I ask.

"You gotta stay alert," VERT reminds, and I try to focus my gaze on the darkness in front of me and my ears on the quiet behind me.

The street numbers are painted on the wall about thirty feet over head, but in the tunnel your conception of space is measured by distance from the exit. For the first ten blocks the walls of the tunnel are filled with graffiti that demands your attention; after that, light, time, and space all become blurred.

We are now deep into the tunnel, and every step takes us further into the unknown. VERT begins to suggest that we take the tunnel all the way to 125th Street. It is 4:20 and we are losing what little daylight is peeking through the grates. I begin to voice my dissent. "No way, let's go back, I don't want to get caught down here at night," I say. VERT is calm but adamant that we continue on.

"We haven't seen FREEDOM's pieces yet," he says.

"Have you ever been all the way through?" I ask.

"No," he says, "but I know you can get out."

"That's reassuring," I say.

Graffiti writers are a mix of artist and outlaw, but they are also thrill-seekers and athletes experienced at taking physical risks and going to extremes to elude pursuing police. I had forgotten all of this about the usually mild-mannered VERT, who in the tunnel had superhero status. I trust him, so I keep walking.

The darkness is powerful, and it begins to feel thick. The crunching underfoot ceases for a moment, so I stop. I had stepped on something soft. Confused, I look down and slowly realize that I am standing on a dead cat. Horrified, and as my eyes adjust further I also catch the frantic scurrying of rats along the wall. This may have been a bad idea, I think to myself. "Come on, let's go," VERT snaps at me.

I focus my eyes ahead and continue walking. Then I notice the orange flickering of fire on the left side of the tunnel about one hundred yards away. This was the first sign of human life that we had recognized.

Someone must have heard us coming because I see a silhouette of a man walking toward the tracks. The tall figure stops and straddles the tracks, striking an impressive pose while waiting to see who had come to visit. When we are in earshot, I say, "Hey, what's up?" The man is friendly and asks if we are painters. VERT says that we are. The man then asks VERT if he has any black paint, and VERT says that we are just here to look.

"I need some black because some track workers went over my face with some bright orange. Actually it's supposed to be my face but it doesn't look like me." He is referring to a mural that we can barely see up in the distance. Bernard, a tall black man with dreadlocks, is a former model, and I recognize him from the photos in Morton's book.

"You're Bernard, right?" I say, introducing myself. "I'm Greg, one of Terry's students."

"Wow. How is Terry? I haven't seen him since New Year's Day. When you see him tell him that I'm moving to Holland House, and tell him to call my voice mail." While we are talking I notice that Bernard has something in his hand that looks like a rock or a potato, which he keeps transferring from hand to hand. What the hell?

"Okay," I say, "I'll tell him. I see him on Tuesday. These are my friends VERT and Sacha."

"Nice to meet you. I'd shake hands but I'm making hamburgers." He says this as if it is the most normal thing in the world and gestures behind him to the fire in the barbecue pit. As we part Bernard says, "Come by anytime—I'm the first house on the left." I peer in the direction he indicates but cannot make out anything more than a large cement wall.

Bernard's comfort with the darkness is reassuring, and his hospitality eases our fears that someone will try to do us harm. Meeting Bernard, the famed Lord of the Tunnel, boosts my confidence, and I press on determined not to let my fear of the dark prevent me from appreciating what the tunnel has to offer.[3]

We are past the halfway point now and I begin to feel an urge to write on the walls. I am proud of myself for venturing into this underworld, and I want others who come after me to know that "Greg was here."

I pick up a rock and start to scratch my name on the wall and VERT and Sacha do the same. There is an organic quality to tagging the walls with the tunnel's own elements, but the tags don't show up very well. As I start to get lost in the wall VERT reminds me that if we keep tagging we won't have enough light to make it out. I quickly put my rock in my pocket and resume my brisk pace.

Then I sense a bright light behind me and turn. An Amtrak passenger train is moving pretty fast right for us, but we have plenty of time to get off of the track and walk safely to the side, close to the tunnel's walls. The train's light cuts a slice through the darkness with no regard for the serene balance of trickling water, dim light, and scurrying rats. As the train approaches, my adrenaline begins to pump and the calm tunnel is transformed into a loud and chaotic space. I turn around to photograph the approaching train and VERT says, "Take my picture when it comes." He is standing no more than five feet from the tracks. The train comes closer and lets out a loud wail of warning to VERT, who jumps just as the train passes. I try to photograph VERT in suspended animation, but I fumble with the camera and miss the shot. Sacha hollers as loud as he can, but he is drowned out by the noise of the train.

The passing of the train purges our anxieties and leaves us with a sense of invincibility. "I hope another one comes," Sacha says seriously. By now we can see the light at the end, and though 5:00 was impending we knew that we would have enough light to make it out, so we slow our pace and begin to pay even closer attention to the graffiti.

FREEDOM has pieces throughout the tunnel, even in the relatively sparse middle sections. His black-and-white pieces on the gray cement walls capture perfectly the context of the tunnel. His aerosol representations of the work of masters, especially Salvador Dalí's melting clock, highlights the surreal feeling of the tunnel.[4]

As we approach the tunnel's exit the world outside greets us rudely. Even before we exit the mouth of the tunnel, corporate America is there to give us a re-briefing. On a Ralph Lauren Polo billboard a blonde woman rests seductively on her side. Like a siren she beckons us to leave the mythical insularity of the darkness.

We hang around the last few feet of the tunnel for a bit, not wanting to venture into the light, then finally exit with a sense of pride and accomplishment. We walk north on the tracks along Riverside Drive until we come to a spot where we can jump the fence. We cross Riverside Drive and walk north to 125th Street right by the Cotton Club.

I thank VERT for taking me to the tunnel, and for insisting that we go all the way through. "Graff has taken me to many cool places that I never would have seen if I didn't have graffiti," he says.

I end the day thinking that graffiti writing is often as much about the process of discovery as it is about actual name painting. This is one of the cherished lessons for the graffiti explorer.

A PILGRIMAGE TO MEK

A Bronx Graffiti Tour

Even though the first generation of graffiti writers clearly predates the emergence of hip hop, for some in the mid-1980s graffiti was just another element of the subculture, along with DJing, break dancing, and eventually rapping.

Hip hop culture was especially efficient in disseminating graffiti to other parts of the country and the world. For MEK, a half-Asian, half-Irish kid growing up in Los Angeles, his first graffiti experience was not on the walls or trains of his city, but on the cardboard boxes that the break dancers would lay out on the sidewalk to provide a smooth dance surface.

> I didn't know about graffiti, until I learned about poppin'. My initial experience with the hip hop scene was through poppin' and breakin'. Then after that it was like all of a sudden I started seeing people with weird stuff on their cardboard, like weird bubble letters. And I'd see kids with Levi's jackets with stuff painted on the back. And then I saw this one Puerto Rican guy, he kept on coming up to Hollywood Boulevard with all kinds of graffiti on his [cardboard]. His name was ZODIAC. He would be on Hollywood Boulevard and he used to do artwork for the break-dancers. He would have markers there and he would bust out all kinds of graffiti for people on their cardboard or whatever. And he got famous for that, and he would tag ZODIAC all over the place. So we used to hook up with him, and he used to do graffiti for us and everything like that. Then SOON came out from New York, and he was on some next shit. He used to go to this place called Pan Pacific Park, and he did a couple pieces there. His pieces were so dope. And this was like 1985 when SOON first arrived on the scene, and SOON just did some damage. And you knew this was no LA shit, this is some real [New York Graffiti] right here. And basically

that guy is the one who mentored a lot of LA writers he's the one who started the crew West Coast Artists. [1]

MEK helps to explain the ways in which subcultures are spread through what sociologists call "micro-social interactions," which are people's relationships at the grassroots level. In the early stages of a subculture, before it can potentially become part of a corporate distribution machine, people carry the culture with them and share it with others through travel and relocation. Cultural studies scholar Tricia Rose has argued that hip hop spreads globally through its use of technology and capitalism, and that this undercuts some of its democratic goals.[2] The experience of MEK and others, however, suggests an organic micro-model of subcultural diffusion, a spreading of knowledge through various communication practices among social actors.

For some music subcultures, like rap, punk, and metal, it is inevitable that their popularity will make them attractive to corporations looking to make profits. Those youths whose first taste of a subculture comes through these macro-processes therefore are not experiencing the subculture in its purest form. Yet it is also the case that there are micro-social interactions occurring at the same time that can reinforce or critique the corporate selling of a subculture. A kid in Los Angeles or Santiago, Chile, might first be inspired by a song or a movie, and this experience may cause her to seek others with more subcultural knowledge, and hence she can eventually learn cultural practices through interacting with other people rather than just buying or consuming a product.

In MEK's case, the relationships he was forming were reinforcing the things he had heard on the radio or read in books. He quickly became enamored with graffiti and learned that fun and fame were to be had by "getting up." Writers utilize different strategies to disseminate their names, and in Los Angeles this meant tagging the buses. Nevertheless, MEK had a plan; he knew his city intimately and became an expert of urban exploration.

We met at the Chameleon Lounge in the East Village in Manhattan, and MEK offered to take me to the Bronx to take some flicks. Even though I have lived in New York City for four years, it was clear that MEK was more knowledgeable than me when it came to Brooklyn and the Bronx.

In most circles MEK, at the age of twenty-four, would be considered a young man with a bright future; however, in the world of hip hop, MEK considers himself an aging master. He has been an active participant in hip hop culture for half his life, and in that time he has honed his skills in various hip hop crafts. In that time he's achieved a solid share of fame and developed associations with crews such as WCA (West Coast Artists), FLY ID, and CBS (California Bomb Squad). Today we were going to see a piece he did with CLARK in the Bronx.

Aboard the Number 2 subway to the Bronx I ask MEK about his crews.

"I was one of the founding West Coast members. In like '89 my boy ROB ONE started hangin' out with this kid EMZ who had moved to LA from the Bronx and was tagging up 'FLY ID.' They were just into bombing, tags and throw-ups, not really pieces, so I was like, whatever. Then I was over at ROB's and I saw this tall black kid and ROB was like, 'that's EMZ.' Me and EMZ started talking and we were cool, so he asked me to start pushing FLY ID. Now there are mad people in FLY ID on both coasts. CLARK is the president of East Coast FLY ID and he puts everyone in his neighborhood in the crew, kids I never even heard of."

"What exactly are the duties of a crew president?" I asked.

"I would say that the job of the president is to perfect a style and then mentor the younger writers in order to carry on the style, but also to build on it so it evolves."

Impressed, I asked, "Were you ever mentored by another writer?"

"Not really. When I was coming up there weren't that many writers around. I learned how to piece by copying the old masters. I figured if I could paint their work, that it would develop my skills. I would copy other writers and change it a bit to make it sort of my own. Like ZEPHYR says about artful biting. You borrow different things from different writers and eventually you develop a style of your own."

"Have you ever acted as the mentor?"

"Sure, I've given kids sketched outlines and stuff," MEK replied. "Mentors also help out with the final outline, which is once you get the piece up on the wall, you do a final outline and that takes skills. If you mess that up the whole piece could be ruined, so the older writer, who has a stake in transmitting the style of crew, will usually do the final outline. Another thing is that when you give an outline to a younger writer, it's best if they copy it completely. Young bucks are always trying to change stuff, but you never learn that way. It's best to master a style before you try to create your own."

We continued our long ride on the Number 2 train. The subway rises above ground in the North Bronx, and here the graffiti rises to the surface, suddenly the gray cement of the buildings' rooftops were bursting with color. As we traveled past them MEK would call out the names of the pieces he recognized. As we sailed by each piece, I jerked my head in the direction MEK referred, sometimes getting only a fleeting glimpse of color, other times making a positive ID. At each stop he enthusiastically recalled what we had seen. "Did you see that WANE piece? That CLARK piece was frrrresh." My senses buzzed with the rush of the train and the energy of the graffiti. The Bronx explodes with graffiti, and I was struck by an intense feeling of respect for the birthplace of hip hop. The importance of the Bronx was not lost on the native Californian either. "This is where it all began," MEK said as the train slowed to a halt at 235th Street.

We bounded down the steps eager to set foot on the sacred ground to begin the hajj to MEK's pieces. There was a sign for the Metro-North train, and MEK beckoned to head in that direction. As we passed Our Lady of Mercy Hospital, MEK said, "That's where I came when I hurt my back. CLARK and I were at this spot and five-O [cops] rolled up just as we were finishing our pieces. We had to jet and jump off this ledge and I fell like twenty feet and hurt my back." As MEK told the story I felt grateful that we were here only to take flicks.

MEK continued with his "raid story," a common tale among writers about how they escaped the police.[3] "We were just finishing our pieces when the cops rolled up on us. They drove right down here on the grass. CLARK had said this spot was chill so I looked at him with surprise as we gathered our stuff and ran. CLARK knew the area well, so I was just blindly following. We got to this spot where we had to jump," said MEK, recollecting his injury. "I paused to look at it and missed and fell right on my back."

MEK had to go to the hospital, but he and CLARK escaped the police.

As we approached the Metro-North stop MEK was telling me he couldn't remember if we were supposed to walk right or left down the tracks to get to the spot where he and CLARK had done their pieces. I wasn't really listening, only following, my eyes fixed on the people standing on the platform and the orange-vested workers across the tracks. I felt like we stuck out like two sore thumbs, but I fed off MEK's nonchalance, and we strode right past the awaiting passengers, jumped down off the platform, and walked north directly along the tracks.

There were black-and-white tags and throw-ups along the brown stone walls lining the east side of the track. In the distance we could see some colors that might have been pieces. "That might be the spot," MEK said, and we walked calmly on this sunny but unseasonably cold day in spring.

I watched my reflection in the black patent leather of my new Air Jordans, while listening to MEK's slightly tinny voice warble over the steady bass crunch of the brown and tan stones underfoot. MEK reflected on his days as a young kid when he was just learning how to DJ.

> There was this Asian kid in my elementary school, Sean, who was from Carson City, which is sorta like the Bronx. This kid was mad quiet and then one day I found out he had turntables. I couldn't believe it because I thought I was the man at my elementary school. I was breakin' and writing graffiti with no competition. I finally went to his house one day and his house was nice. Sure enough he had two turntables and a vinyl mat for breakin'. He started to cut and scratch,[4] and right there I decided to get tables. From that day I got serious about hip hop and was interested in it more than just as a way to pick up girls. You asked me once what I would've done if I hadn't discovered graffiti, and I'm telling you, if I hadn't met Sean I'd probably be locked up or something. With so many people around me doing shit like dealing it would've been easy to take that path.

When MEK discovered graffiti in the late 1980s it was already associated with hip hop. For some, being part of hip hop culture means pursuing all four elements: writing, DJing, breaking, and rapping. For others, graffiti and rap are only loosely related.

We got to the spot where we had seen what looked like pieces and found nothing of note. "It must be down the other way," MEK said, and we turned around and walked back the way we came. Again, when we got to the platform I was nervous that the workers would say something, but they didn't seem to notice us walking down the tracks and jumping up on the platform.

We exited the Metro-North area and walked down a path on the east side of the tracks that MEK recognized. "This is the spot where CLARK and I got chased by the cops," he said. We walked down a paved path that flanked the bank of the Bronx River. The brown stone wall lining the path was covered with silver "straight-letter" pieces, which lie somewhere between a throw-up and a graffiti masterpiece. The straight-letter piece takes a little longer than a throw-up to complete because of the more technical lettering and the addition of more colors, usually three or four. The form is also quite legible and is used to get your name out. MEK and CLARK had done silver pieces at the beginning of the wall.

MEK kept telling stories of his past as we walked along the path underneath a bridge. The bridge's walls are arched, and the big colorful

MEK and CLARK, FLY ID (C.ID), straight-letter pieces, Bronx.

pieces by SIEN 5, STAK, KASE II, and others reflected perfectly on the surface of the water. I paused for a moment, struck by the strangeness of graffiti in this almost country setting. I think about the irony that something as "urban" as graffiti writing would lead its followers to discover the city's hidden rural areas.

We walked back up to White Plains Road to check out the pieces in this area, known as the Jamaican Bronx. The first graff we stumbled upon was a 1993 production by C.O.D. crew. MEK and I took pictures of this collaborative effort by DAZE, WANE, and DASH. Even though this work was three years old it was untouched by other writers. "They got mad respect for graffiti in the Bronx," MEK said. "No one goes over pieces here."

About three blocks away MEK got excited as we came upon an orange and black piece that was so hot that it was what writers call a "burner." The piece was about twenty feet long and more than six feet high. The letter style was sharp and clean and angled in such a way as to indicate motion. The connections between the letters gave the appearance that it was a single whole. "That's my man RELM and that shit is frrrresh." MEK started to break down his friend's piece for me. Like a lot or writers he is highly critical of lots of graffiti, but when he comes across something that he thinks is original, his enthusiasm is infectious. "Check how he blended the colors, check the outline, and he's got like vents in that thing with smoke coming out. Daaaaamn." Here, my appreciation was aided by my tutor's keen

RELM, Bronx, circa 1996.

eye, and we kept getting deeper and deeper into it as MEK analyzed the numerous elements that accounted for the effectiveness of the piece. The orange fill outlined in black gave the piece an aggressive feel, almost like it was trying to jump off the wall, while the arrows and the smoke gave the impression of speed and movement, pure energy.

The fact that we could randomly stumble upon something with this much beauty and feeling is one of the truly populist qualities of graffiti. We didn't use the Internet or buy a magazine, and it required no cover charge and no bouncers to get past. It's just there to be viewed by anyone, for free. This aspect of graffiti is sometimes lost as so much technology is caught up in the documentation and dissemination of graffiti. There are endless websites devoted to documenting and recording the progression of the movement, but these fail in comparison to seeing the work live.

As a subculture, graffiti is unique in that the folks who do it are underground and secretive and are essentially only concerned with what other writers think about their work. However, we cannot forget that this work takes place in public. This obviously is where the controversy also lies with respect to graffiti, but sometimes graffiti writers make public art. The idea that writers are doing something for themselves that elicits a positive emotional response from certain members of the population is amazing. This subculture has the power to inspire on a truly democratic level. What is lost sometimes in the cacophony of the debate over whether graffiti is art or vandalism is that when it's art, it is free art. You don't need money, or special knowledge, or the right outfit, or a car, or an ID to see it. This is why the graffiti subculture has inspired such a diversity of young people. It is also why the culture continues to evolve and to progress, and why some people who become fascinated by it make entire lives out of serendipitous moments.

LEGAL GRAFFITI

Contemporary Permission Spots

Graffiti writing in its purest form is about making a name for oneself by any means. For writers this means getting up enough to get noticed and then following up and building a reputation. This takes dedication, courage, and guile, as well as having "style," the writers' term for artistic skill.

In the post-train era legal walls have become essential to the progression of the art form. Piecing with style requires more time and more supplies than tags and throw-ups, so piecing illegally often exposes writers to way too much risk from the police. Therefore, many graffiti pieces done today are done on legal walls on which writers have been granted permission to paint by the building owner. Legal walls allow writers to take their time, and this results in some really good art. The art done on legal walls, often called

REAS legal wall, SoHo.

STAN 153, Graffiti Hall of Fame, Harlem, 1998.

"productions," is usually a collaborative effort involving the work of a handful of artists in the same crew. Legal walls allow writers to showcase their talents and even enjoy creating art together in the light of day. This process is also one of the few times that writers can socialize with each other.

Since the beginning of the movement some photographers, gallery owners, journalists, and community activists have treated writers as artists whose creativity should be encouraged, rather than as destructive vandals. Castleman documents the work of Hugo Martinez, who, as a sociology major at City College, in 1972 formed an organization of graffiti writers called United Graffiti Artists (UGA), which provided artists with canvases and opportunities to paint legally. This is not to suggest that writers cease all illegal work as soon as they begin to paint legally, but it is important to point out that graffiti is not always illegal. UGA lasted only a few years, but it had an enduring impact on many of the youth who participated in it, as they began to experience a sense of self-worth and confidence that they could become successful adults.[1]

Even at the height of painting illegal murals on subways (1973–85), there were writers who divided their time between legal and illegal work. In 1980 Ray Rodriguez founded the Graffiti Hall of Fame at 106th and Park Avenue in East Harlem. Ray was not a writer but a community activist and art lover who wanted a place to let writers showcase their talents. The Graffiti Hall of Fame was a tourist spot for writers and art lovers from all over the world.

In *Spraycan Art,* Prigoff writes about the impact of this spot: "The Graffiti Hall of Fame became an inspiration for youth across the country and around the world. Local 'Halls of Fame' were designated in such far-flung places as Crocker Park in Daly City, California, a park tunnel in Amsterdam, Holland, and a demolished city block near the Stalingrad section of Paris, France."[2] To this day the Graffiti Hall of Fame is still repainted yearly, but only by an exclusive group of masters.

After Prigoff's book came out, writers in even more cities, including Washington and Denver, also established their own halls of fame. Some of these spots were legal; others were just secret illegal spots where writers could paint safely without fear of arrest.[3]

As the train era came to a close, writers began to seek new spaces to paint, and this inevitably forced writers aboveground onto the walls of the city. Writers out to bomb had to become expert urban explorers, as they turned the city into a concrete jungle gym, climbing and scaling new heights to make their mark. Some of the early kings were writers like JOZ, JOSH 5, and EASY, who were said to have painted on every roll-down gate in the city.[4]

Many writers who had established reputations sought ways to alleviate the stress of illegal writing while continuing to pursue graffiti art. These writers looked for legal walls to ply their craft. Some of the first aboveground legal graffiti murals were memorial walls. These R.I.P. murals, as they are sometimes called, are documented in Martha Cooper and James Sciorra's book *R.I.P.: Memorial Wall Art* (1994). This trend was started organically by writers who painted in memory of their friends, but soon writers began to paint memorials for hire for other members of the community. These

CHICO, East Village, 1999.

murals are sophisticated artistic productions, often with a life-like portrait of the person that passed. Memorial walls are a ubiquitous and generally accepted form of graffiti art that many New Yorkers are familiar with.

Nowadays, most aerosol memorial art is not a spontaneous reflection of grief but a business transaction between the artist and the loved one's family. I ran into CHICO, a well-known muralist who has painted many memorial walls. He was painting a mural on 9th Street and Second Avenue for a grocery store. He was up on a ladder applying brown spray paint to a brick-red wall. He had already completed the left side with a realistic aerosol rendition of some fruit and the words "OPEN 24 HOURS" and "ATM INSIDE." I was curious about how the wall would turn out, so I said to his back, "Do you have a sketch?"

He turned around and said, "No," but paused, opening the door to further questions.

"How much are you getting paid?" I asked.

"Fifteen hundred dollars. That's eleven hundred for me and four hundred for paint."

"What about memorial walls?"

"Four hundred for paint, and two to three hundred dollars more, depending on whether or not I do a portrait with airbrush."

"How can people get in contact with you?" I asked.

"I got a business card." CHICO fished one out of his back pocket, sort of folded it so it would fly better, and tossed it down.

I thanked him and was on my way.

Even when they don't generate money for the writers, painting memorials can be a very positive experience. A memorial wall becomes a public performance of graffiti art, as well as providing many in the community space to come together to share collective grief. In a recent email exchange KEZAM, a writer from Australia and current Yale graduate student in sociology, talked about his experience painting a memorial wall for two people he didn't know but was able to get a sense of through this community ritual:

> I've only done one memorial wall. It was a joint wall for TWITCH and JROCK out in Williamsburg. It's an interesting experience as a writer. I did it just because I wanted to paint. But as I was doing it, a lot of the community came out to watch. A lot of the people who did watch, knew the two people that had died. At one point TWITCH's mom

came out to see what was going on and how the wall was coming out. A lot of his friends also came by. Some of them could show me what he looked like as they had had his image tattooed since his passing. As I was doing this wall and interacting with various people, it dawned on me that I was no longer just creating some interesting aesthetic forms, but producing something that had deep meaning to a lot of people.[5]

Cooper and Sciorra claim in their book that this phenomenon is in part due to the entrepreneurial spirit of graffiti artists, who developed this medium as a way of garnering some commercial success for their work. Many of these entrepreneurs were young fathers looking to make some relatively quick cash using their aerosol skills for commercial signage. Small-business owners in the Bronx, Brooklyn, Queens, and the Lower East Side often do not have the money to hire professional sign painters and instead pay graffiti writers to paint their walls to attract customers. These walls also give the stores a certain amount of status, as many of the writers are local heroes.

The group of writers in TATS CRU have established themselves as the "Kings of Murals," and they operate a successful business as commercial graffiti artists. They have done numerous memorial walls; promotional campaigns for Coke, M&Ms, and Snapple; and commercial art for schools, hospitals, and health care groups. TATS CRU have painted motor homes for health care providers, whose vehicles allow them to bring care to people in the community.[6]

The writers in TATS CRU, BIO, BG, NICER, all began their careers by painting illegally on the sides of New York City subways, and today they operate as successful commercial artists. They have inspired other writers from across the country to pursue similar goals. The Art Crimes website (www.graffiti.org), which is the first and most extensive graffiti site, lists more than sixty artists who work as muralists for hire.

Suffice to say that there is a market for legal graffiti, and in some ways it has become a big business. Advertisers use graffiti tactics, saturating walls and lampposts with stickers, but also use actual aerosol art to develop sophisticated branding campaigns. The Boston company Alt Terrain specializes in having writers paint legal murals as public performance. According to the company's website, these "brand events," which cost between $7,500 and $12,500, are "live graffiti performances" that consist of "talented graffiti artists creating a brand advertising mural."[7]

Legal Spots

With all this commerce, the question of graffiti as a pure expressive medium unencumbered by capitalism has become moot. This does not mean, however, that there aren't writers who love to paint without the desire to be paid and for the most part do so legally. Writers search the city for spots they like and then attempt to get permission from the building owner. This usually requires showing a portfolio and explaining what type of production is planned. "Permission walls are pretty cool," says KEZAM. But he also warns:

> You are more or less guaranteed to have the vandal squad make an appearance—so you better have permission slips from the owner of the property. You also want the owner to be available by phone, as some vandal squad members will go out of their way to contact the property owner to check the validity of the permission slip. There are many writers who have been arrested even though they had permission. They are usually released later when everything is clarified, though. As far as art goes, permission walls have been really good as they enable writers to take their time and produce more detailed and planned-out work.

There are also spots specifically set aside for aerosol art, often as the result of some sort of community activism, which give writers a chance to develop artistic and creative skills. In New York City this spot is 5 Pointz, located in Long Island City, Queens. Today 5 Pointz is run by two writers, MERES and NIC ONE; however, this spot was originally called the Phun Phactory and was started by Pat Delillo in 1995. Delillo started out as an anti-graffiti vigilante, but the more graffiti he was exposed to the more he realized that he liked pieces.[8]

Delillo had a vision that he could help writers channel their energy into something more socially acceptable by giving them legal wall space to explore their creative talents. The building he chose was a warehouse at 45-14 Davis Street in Long Island City that was covered in illegal graffiti. Because this warehouse is visible from the elevated Number 7 train, it had been a longtime favorite for writers. Pat convinced the building owner that if they could replace the tags with pieces, they could provide an outlet for neighborhood youth and make their building more presentable in the eyes of the public. Anyone who has traveled from Manhattan out to a Mets game or to the Billie Jean King National Tennis Center has witnessed this explosion of color as the train comes out of the dark tunnel.

These legal graffiti spots have dismantled some of the controversy over graffiti vandalism. While some of the most ardent anti-graffiti activists worry that providing kids with a place to paint encourages more illegal graffiti, local Queens websites list 5 Pointz as one of the main attractions for tourists to visit in the neighborhood.[9]

The prevalence of these spots in cities all over the world, combined with the World Wide Web, has added another path to fame that doesn't include saturating city walls illegally with a name. Many writers who piece do so by painting legal walls and then send the photos to the numerous graffiti websites. Kids who want to see graffiti turn on their computers and scroll through flicks from the top writers from around the world. The really hot pieces create a buzz, and some of these writers are then invited to go to the various legal wall spots in other parts of the world. Fame comes from getting your flicks viewed and getting your work talked about in chat rooms. This fame occurs on a truly global level as writers, especially young writers, flock to www.graffiti.org to see the latest pieces from Germany, Spain, South Africa, Chile, Europe, and the United States.

STYLE POINTS

ESPO's Brooklyn Mural

Espo started writing graffiti as a teenager in Philadelphia, where he learned the fundamentals of what are called "prints," or stylized signatures: "tall prints," a name written as tall as you can reach; "rally prints," the name written over and over; and "wickets" (or "wickeds"), a type of writing that requires eight beats per letter. All of these forms play a role in the development of style. ESPO showed early artistic promise, but it wasn't until he honed his relationship with SUROC, a Philly originator, that he began to develop a unique style of his own. SUROC was well-versed in graffiti styles, but he also read postmodern theory and studied modern art. He taught ESPO that it was important for writers to know about European artists like Marcel Duchamp and John Heartfield. ESPO writes in his book that "Duchamp upended the perception of what was considered art and who was considered an artist. With Heartfield it was the way he used photomontage and collage to criticize the Nazi regime of his native Germany eloquently and effectively."[1]

ESPO credits SUROC for inspiring him not just to paint his name effectively, but to add a thematic component to his graffiti pieces. Even while ESPO was fully immersed in the subcultural world of graffiti, he wanted to contextualize his work in the larger traditions of art movements and pop culture. Since moving to New York in 1994 ESPO had tested some of the ideas he learned from his mentor, becoming, as he calls it, a "high art vandal."

But ESPO is far from a pretentious art snob. Being a top-notch graffiti writer requires work, and in New York ESPO learned his work ethic from REVS. Despite REVS's many achievements in his twenty-plus-year graffiti career—from roller tags, to wheat-pasted flyers, to welded metal sculptures, to an underground tunnel autobiography—REVS is still about work. Although he has been written up in *Artforum* and *Juxtapose* magazines, he has for the most part shunned the art scene and continues to forgo sleep in the service of his craft. ESPO too has learned about putting in work. In the summer of 1997 REVS picked him up at 5 A.M. to paint a spot in Brooklyn.

Flatbush Field Notes

It had been a long time since I'd seen ESPO paint, and I was excited that he'd invited me to witness his process. The spot, located off Rutland Road in Flatbush, has a small soccer stadium with a running track behind it. The track is lined on the south, east, and north sides by cement walls about twelve feet high that are perfect for painting murals. ESPO told me that REVS had secured some sort of verbal permission to paint, but the fact that the painters could not be seen from the street meant that the issue probably wouldn't come up.

It was 4 P.M. when I arrived. Each writer had been allotted a space approximately twelve feet high and twenty feet wide. Gone are the days when teenage writers would load up backpacks and shopping bags with spray paint and sneak into the subways to paint. Such guerilla attacks are more rare these days. Instead, ESPO and REVS operate with the precision of the modern military. REVS's pick-up truck has been fitted to hold ladders, poles, rollers, and paint—lots of paint. There are two five-gallon buckets of white primer and milk crate after milk crate of spray paint. Despite the collective nature of mural production, each writer is responsible for obtaining his or her own paint, though sometimes common colors such as blacks and whites will be shared.

Before a single can of spray paint is aimed at the wall, the surface must be primed with a fresh coat of white exterior house paint that writers call "bucket paint." This process is called "buffing," a reference to the chemical process the Metropolitan Transportation Authority (MTA) employed in the 1970s to clean the subways. Writers paint white over the old, worn-out graffiti for both aesthetic and practical reasons. A clean wall gives the artist a blank surface to work with, in addition to saving paint. Cement walls are porous and tend to soak up spray paint, thus requiring more for adequate coverage.

Sometimes a younger, less-established writer will be given the job of rolling the white on the wall and carrying supplies, but usually writers will "buff" their own walls. Some have perfected this practice of painting with rollers and will use them to fill-in large areas of their pieces or even to paint massive letters, a technique that REVS and his then-partner COST pioneered in the early 1990s.

I walked out onto the green grass in the middle of the track and was surrounded by color. The south and east walls were almost completed and resonated with the pride of newness. Directly in front of me, in the middle of the east wall, was a piece with curious-looking letters that I soon realized were ESPO's. I was about 150 yards away and ESPO's letters were reeling me in. I noticed his familiar walk and whistled to get his attention. When I got closer to him I offered wild praise, thanking him for allowing me to witness this project in motion. ESPO flashed a confident smile and said, "I ain't going for second place."

ESPO's unique style was apparent even amid this conglomeration of some of graffiti's finest. Even the way that ESPO used his allotted space on the wall contrasted markedly with the other writers. Many writers will do "Top to Bottoms," a term that refers to pieces that stretch from the top to the bottom of the train or the wall. ESPO, however, had a plan for the whole wall that contextualizes his letters, rather than laying them on top of an elegant background. ESPO's letters were centered on the space, focusing the viewers gaze and allowing for the characters and background to complement the letters in the piece. "The theme for this wall," said ESPO, "is a Crib Bust. That's when the cops come to your house and bust you."[2] ESPO told me that he envisioned two cops on each side of his piece interrogating it under bright lights. So far he had completed the E-S-P-O in the center of the wall and the overweight cop seated to the left of it pointing an accusing finger at the piece.

ESPO walked back to his piece and I sat back in the grass, soaking up the evening sun and the vibe of the artists relishing a chance to savor their creativity collectively. As ESPO tightened up his character I took the opportunity to check my surroundings. The south wall was beaming with fresh new productions by two crews I didn't recognize. "Productions" are murals done by a group of artists in a crew on a large surface, usually with a common theme.

When writers paint permission pieces they are usually engaged in a collective process of art-making. There were about seven writers, each of whom had an equal portion of the wall. To ESPO's left was a piece that ZEUS and SHOW had completed earlier in the day. The next spot over, SP ONE and TAB were hard at work on a piece that had trains in it. Next to them REVS was painting a wild-looking piece that read "Charger '69" in homage to his car. In the corner on the north wall, PEEK was working on a silver and dark-green piece in which the letters looked like metal axes. This piece was big and covered almost the entire allotted space on the wall.

To ESPO's right, JOEY and FUEL were busy working on their piece, which had huge, straight letters. In the center of it was a rendering of Mayor Rudolph Giuliani pulling a stool out from under a black-hooded graffiti writer with a noose around his neck. When FUEL first started talking to me about the piece, he was a little frustrated with how his characters were turning out, but as he talked more about it he convinced himself it was acceptable, and from then on his confidence grew. "We're running this whole wall," he chided in ESPO's direction, indicating that they thought their piece was the best. "Pleeeeeeeease," was Steve's only response. FUEL went back to the wall, twisted the cap off of his spray can, and aggressively began to add polish to his characters while JOEY worked on the letters. By using paper and cardboard as stencils, they gave their characters extremely clean edges. FUEL also used the outline of a masking tape roll to paint the curves in the rope. This technique, if done poorly, will make the piece seem choppy, but JOEY and FUEL are quite proficient in this practice.

Graffiti art is first and foremost about letter form, and ESPO, like all graffiti masters, exhibits extreme control over the shape of his letters. ESPO's work is symmetrical and balanced. This piece, like some of his others, had a distinct center axis where the "S" and "P" came together. The "E" and "O" on both ends of ESPO looked very similar and gave the piece balance.

PEEK, Flatbush, Brooklyn.

REVS, "Charger 69," Flatbush, Brooklyn.

ESPO doesn't merely paint his letters but constructs them as if they were made out of giant metal tubes; care must be taken to balance the weight evenly throughout the structure. The letters in the structure form a solid whole, with a negligible amount of negative space. ESPO rarely utilizes the iconic arrows or stars, called designs, which became part of the graffiti lexicon during the golden era of pieces on the subways.

"I took all the arrows and shit out of my pieces a long time ago. Some kids in Philly got with it, but others can't get away from it. They need to do something different. 'That's New York, that's not your culture,' I tell them "You learned that from a book," ESPO said, referring to the legions of kids outside of New York who learned their styles from *Subway Art* and *Spraycan Art*.

"Did you do an outline for this?" I asked.

"Only this," he said, handing me a quickly drawn sketch that showed only a slight resemblance to the piece on the wall. The sketch hadn't been colored and there were no notes or guidelines describing the colors. "I knew that I wanted to use purple in the fill-in and a forest-green outline, but that's all I had planned." ESPO only had a rough idea of what he wanted to paint. He says he likes to let the piece come to him as he gets to know the space, which is also why ESPO's work always seems to fit into the context of the environment. "This is gonna be my best piece yet," he said as he put on his protective mask and reached into his pocket for his yellow rubber dishwashing glove.

He was the only writer that day wearing a mask or gloves. "This shit is serious. I don't believe these guys. REVS, SP, they both have a cough and they don't even smoke; other writers have trouble with their kidneys. I'm protecting myself. I don't want to get to a point where I'm really onto something and then have stop because it's affecting my health."[3]

After ESPO had completed the highlights on the seated character, he began to work on the second character on the right side of the piece. Writers call anything that is not a letter, from a bug to realistic humans, a "character." This term hails back to the 1970s and 1980s, when writers would incorporate the characters of comic artists' like Vaughn Bodé into their pieces. Writers also made famous the "b-boy" character, which is a cartoonish figure striking a break-dance pose or holding hip hop icons like large radios. ESPO seems intent on developing his own cast of characters that are more life-like.

ESPO held his can of yellow to the wall and started to sketch freehand as if he were using a pencil. In five minutes it looked like a person, in ten minutes it looked like a cop, and in thirty minutes it looked like a man who had something on his mind.

Now that ESPO had the elements in place, his energy started to dwindle. It was 8 P.M. and the light was beginning to fade. Despite twelve hours of work ESPO conceded that he would have to return another day to finish. He stepped back to take it in when he noticed the other writers assembled in front of the north wall, which had only tags and a few throwups on it. ESPO walked over to join the other writers who were catching tags on the wall. Each writer would take the can of black and walk slowly up to the wall and paint their tag. As the writers continued to perform for each other the stakes got higher and the competition more intense. PEEK brought a ladder over and one by one the writers climbed the ladder and painted their tags. ESPO climbed up and caught a tag and then walked back to work on his piece, but REVS, SP ONE, and JOEY couldn't help themselves as the ladder allowed them free reign on the space that the other tags couldn't touch. One tag became two, then four, as they moved the ladder on down the wall. Finally they'd had enough and returned to their respective wall spots and started to gather up their paint.

There was at least an hour of daylight left. ESPO, though tired, pushed himself to get more finished before quitting. Then he turned and motioned for me to come closer. I walked up to the wall and ESPO held a can of black spray paint in his hand. He outlined an area underneath his letters and said, "Here, you're going to fill this in."

"How?" I asked, nervous about holding a can so close to his work.

"Just do however you feel comfortable." He passed me the can. "Wait," he said, taking the can of Rustoleum back and removing the comfort cap, which he replaced with a smaller white cap.

Writers use caps of varying size to control the width of paint. Krylon comes stock with caps that spray an approximately one-centimeter width. These are sometimes referred to as outline caps or Liquitex Tips and are used for detail and outline work. Rustoleum comes with caps that spray two-centimeter width, and writers will often replace this cap in order to get a cleaner line. Three-, four-, and five-centimeter-width caps, commonly referred to as "fat caps," are used for filling in large areas quickly and must be obtained from other sources. In the early days of writing, SUPERKOOL, the inventor of the first piece, discovered that the caps from other aerosol products such as oven cleaners and spray starch widened the width of the paint, but today German companies specialize in supplying writers with a large array of caps.[4]

There are also six-centimeter fat caps, as well as outline caps that are smaller than one centimeter and are used for fine detail work. The spray can also be controlled by how much paint is in the can. Writers will put aside half-full cans and use them for detail work because the paint comes out under less pressure and is easier to control.

"Here," ESPO said and handed the can back to me. I started to paint in the prescribed area. I was nervous and hoped that I wouldn't ruin the piece. I stayed far away from the letters, but I was applying the paint way too thick and I ran out of paint with only a third of the area covered. I was embarrassed but ESPO just pulled out another can of black Rustoleum and this time showed me how to do it. "Try putting it on in two coats instead of one." As he said this his arm whipped across the wall in clean rhythmic strokes, while depressing the nozzle in short bursts rather than just holding it down like I had done earlier. I imitated ESPO's method and this time it was fun. I swung my arm back and forth to the beats pumping out of ESPO's boom box and the paint went on smooth and consistent. Using this method I was able to cover the remaining two-thirds with only one can. ESPO's goal was simply to get the space covered while he worked on his character, but it had the effect of providing me with first-hand knowledge of the amount of technical skill required to paint effectively with aerosol.

ESPO, Flatbush, Brooklyn, 1997.

The simplest task turned out to be rather difficult, furthering my appreciation for those who have done elaborate work in this medium.[5]

The sun had set on this day of painting and it was time to pack up the ladders and other paint supplies. By the time everything was cleaned up it was nearing 9 P.M. "You must be exhausted," I said to ESPO as we lugged paint back to REVS's truck.

"I had my adrenaline pumping for a long time because of the piece, but now I'm finally tired."

Inclement weather prevented ESPO from returning as quickly as he would have liked. He finally finished the wall a few days later, and though I was unable to attend, I later made a special mission to view the completed work.

When I got to the spot, there was no question that ESPO had lived up to his own challenge. Across the top of the piece he had painted a mock Dick Tracy cartoon titled "Dick Tricky."

ESPO told me that this work was pure graffiti entertainment—and not only because his chosen subject matter, cops, is a constant source of humor and derision among writers. The piece operated on three distinct levels of graffiti. The letters broke from the time-tested standard of outline, fill-in, and 3-D, resulting in a piece that was original and fresh. The characters were a testament to the realism that can be achieved with aerosol. The comic strip provided the editorial section of this work, allowing ESPO to communicate his message in a more sophisticated manner than simply painting slogans next to his piece.

ESPO's editorial comments were aimed first at writers. In the first panel he wrote, "Crime Doers Notebook #1: Never Admit Anything." He proceeded to show how the police will use questioning tactics to try and get writers to betray each other. Here ESPO was trying to articulate a code of conduct among writers and educate them on the perils of police interrogations.

As I stepped back from this work to take in all of these elements, I began to notice that the work had a triangular feel to it. The spotlight shined through the comic, putting "ESPO" under intense scrutiny, and if those lines were extended they would form a triangle enclosing the characters, the letters, and the comic strip. Here ESPO used a design technique that reinforced his tripartite thematic.

In this painting ESPO once again challenged the public to see his work as both crime and art, pushing the issue of illegality outside of its simple polarities. In this work ESPO had given freely of himself, choosing to stay away from the posturing that pollutes a lot of graffiti's power. In this work, which requires no insider knowledge to appreciate, ESPO had also given mainstream audiences something they could understand about the ethos of graffiti culture.

ILLUSTRATING CRIMINAL

Split PSOUP

PSOUP was the first writer I met, but he did not reveal this to me at the time. Dave, as I knew him, worked with me at Angelika Kitchen long before VERT and others came aboard. Angelika is an organic, vegetarian restaurant that has consistently employed hardcore-straightedge, vegan kids, and Dave was typical in this sense. Our first meeting, however, did not go well. The first time we worked together we had an argument, and I thought that Dave was just another punk. We eventually developed a good working relationship, but he soon left to go to art school. When he came back we developed a friendship, and I convinced him to do a word in my blackbook.

Dave is one of the few graffiti writers that I have talked to who disagrees with my thesis that participation in graffiti culture can have a positive impact on one's adult life. He thinks in general that graffiti is for "fuck ups" who drink too much and get in too many fights. Despite his many achievements—Dave has a BFA from SUNY Purchase in upstate New York and an MFA from Yale University—he does not credit graffiti. He currently lives and works in Brooklyn, where he makes art and is represented by various galleries in Chelsea. He feels that he has achieved these things in spite of his graffiti work, and his artwork does not give any indication that he was a very creative, talented graffiti writer.

Dave is one of those guys who is prone to rants that he gives with a twinkle in his eye, and I'm never quite sure if what he's saying is what he believes or what he wants me to believe he believes. When I looked at what he had done in the blackbook I was confused. He had chosen the page with "criminal" at the bottom. The piece is red, purple, yellow, and green and done with markers that give the impression of watercolors. The letters are in a thin and wispy calligraphy that for me is nearly indecipherable. Even though he says that he was trying to do a simple style to

PSOUP, illustration of the page for "Criminal" from the author's blackbook.

accommodate the fact that it would not be seen only by graffiti writers, I cannot see how this piece says "criminal" and have no idea what it does say. Dave is not smug, but he clearly enjoys this fact.

> If I do a blackbook that only writers see I rock insane handstyles that even my boys take like ten minutes to figure out. I want kids to try and figure out what it says and figure out the intricacies, but for your book, which non-writers will also read, I did the basic wording across the top so that everybody knows what I'm talking about and do a letter style that I like to do.

I look closer above the piece at the clearer script and it says, "If Jack Kevorkien [*sic*] is a criminal I'm proud to be 1 too." I then realize that instead of criminal the piece says "KEVORKIEN." Comparing petty vandalism to assisted suicide is a bit much, but PSOUP is punk rock in all the right ways and certainly not averse to hyperbole.

> As a criminal I think I have a high degree of morals. Writers talk all the time that they won't write graffiti on churches, on private property, on people's houses. I try to stick to that. Once in a while I would stray, you know—like when I was sixteen or something, I didn't give a shit,

I wrote on people's cars, I wrote on anything I could get my hands on. I was a sixteen-year-old fuck up, but as I matured, my criminality matured. The morals that I formed tied into being a criminal, like if I rack [steal] I try not to rack from a mom and pop store, you try to go for the big-time corporate places that are forcing all the other places to close. I'm not down with the corporations. But you know, if I was really interested in changing society I would be reading the paper and getting super political. I can't use the word immoral to describe graffiti, because morals are completely relative—each culture, each society, everybody has different morals. I think according to my set of morals that it's not wrong to write graffiti, but I think it's wrong to scribble your name the exact same way without pushing any boundaries. I just think that is wrong to keep doing the same thing.

Dave begins by suggesting that graffiti hasn't been that useful for him, but when he gets caught up in a story he clearly reveals a passion for the adventure of it.

From graffiti I learned how to be a good lookout, and I learned how to look somewhat inconspicuous. I learned a lot of skills that I can't really use. I learned that I like to cut loose and go nuts as long as I'm not physically hurting somebody. I think a lot of people need that. For me, my release was like climbing forty foot billboards by myself, or riding through ill neighborhoods by myself, like everything I did by myself, rooftops, tunnels, crazy shit. That's how I stayed sane. I was a bike messenger during the day and insane tension builds up and how do I release it? I go out and I bomb all night on my bike. You know it's like my answer back to them. Fuck them, they want to run me over in their bus, their taxicabs? Fuck them, I'm gonna bomb the shit out of this stuff. That was my release and it's gone. And I notice it man, I get stressed and it just builds, I don't have a release anymore.

I think if you write graffiti through your teenage years and into your early twenties, you have a totally different view of the world. You definitely haven't lived a sheltered life. By writing on the world you've also seen what you've been writing on. If you're in the South Bronx at two in the morning to hit some highway, you're still seeing where you park your car to paint the highway, whether you're from the suburbs or whatever. We were from Connecticut, we used to come in, fifteen-year-olds painting highways in the Bronx by ourselves at two in the morning, cars whizzing by, shit like that. I don't know too many other fifteen-year-olds from Connecticut that would even go to the city. I saw shit that none of my peers saw who weren't writers. When I was seventeen I walked through the Bronx River at 238th Street. When I was nineteen I'd walked miles and miles of underground subway track, and I painted so many different subway lines. I know how the trains work, I know so much shit that nobody my age should know unless they're a conductor. It's insane—when I'm riding the subway and we're in a tunnel I look out the window and I find not only the graffiti interesting, but also the signals and the construction work—all the different shit in there, I find it all so interesting.

Despite the fact that Dave disagrees with the idea of the subculture career, it is clear that some aspects of graffiti culture have been important to him. He sometimes sounds like a recovered addict when he talks about graffiti—he even went so far as to pass his name on to another writer to keep himself from writing—but a year later REVS convinced PSOUP to come out of retirement to join him in his subway tunnel exploits. But eventually Dave was able to leave writing altogether and concentrate on fine art.

These days he works as a professional artist and has had successful gallery shows. It's hard to trace the graffiti influences in his paintings, but it is clear that his graffiti experience was important to his development as an artist and as a person, even though his relationship to writing is complicated.

Well, I feel like I had something, and I'm glad I had it because I loved it and I still love it. But I hate it and I say that I wish I never did it, but I know that I loved it. I know that I did stuff that meant something to me at the time and still means something to me and that most people will never do in their lifetime. I'm glad about all that.

AME

Bombing Styles, Inventing Self

The stereotype of the graffiti bomber is of a hardcore writer addicted to the thrill of the chase, the excitement of getting up, and the fun of exploring the city, perhaps even high on marijuana, malt liquor, cocaine, crack, or whatever else might be available. Most bombers are bad-asses.[1] As noted earlier, most are men, with the exception of CLAW, MISS 17, JAKEE, and a few others, who get up with the best of the men. And, in fact, many of these guys are hard-drinking, drug-abusing, fearless dudes who love to fight and who go to any extent to get their names in the best spots. Getting up and staying up is incredibly difficult in this city. There are cops and other writers to deal with, and those who paint on the sides of highways must contend with passing cars. Couple this with the fact that most bombers are on the lookout for the spots that provide the most visibility—which are, of course, also the most dangerous. Every single night writers are standing on six-inch precipices on the tops of buildings, ropes around their waists, partner holding on, while they paint a two-color throw-up. To do this once would give someone stories for a lifetime, but this would only earn you derision from other writers if that was your only claim to fame.

Even if you're not scared of heights, there is trouble in the form of beef. When you start to challenge the reigning champs, there's going to be some not-so-friendly competition. Dudes are going to go over your name, write in your spots, talk negatively about you, and try and get you to give up. How you respond will determine your legacy. Did you show heart, or did you punk out? If you meet these challenges, both physically and with consistent painting on the street, your reputation is solidified and you can hoist a king's crown. Stories will be told of your exploits and you can slow down a bit, because now, you're a star. You have earned fame and respect, both of which are a currency that can be invested. Some folks fade away, but others, like CLAW, EARSNOT, and DASH SNOW, have turned this fame into something tangible. CLAW designs clothes; EARSNOT designs clothes and sneakers and makes art; DASH SNOW's Polaroids of his decadent exploits have been shown in the Whitney Biennial, and he gets mentioned in the same sentence with photographers like Nan Goldin, who photographed her crew of heroin-abusing art hipsters in the 1970s.[2]

AME has some of these qualities. He got his fame over about a three-year period and then slowed down considerably. For some, this life is just too chaotic and destructive to continue. When I first met AME he was a hard-charging graffiti kid, consumed day and night by a fierce will to get up and get noticed and to have fun, but today he's less interested in getting up and is reflective and articulate about graffiti and what it means.

AME grew up in Peekskill, a town in Westchester County, New York. His mother is from Latvia and came to the states as a young girl to escape Soviet domination. She was the only one in her family who could speak English, and AME says she used to accompany her grandfather to job interviews. AME's father is German, English, and Native American. When AME was in the fourth grade his older brother started writing graffiti so he tagged along. His first tag name was SLASH, but AME says that then he didn't even know that the purpose of writing your name was to get fame. When he was young, he never took graffiti seriously and spent most of his time skateboarding.

AME finally learned what graffiti was all about and spent his high school years coming into the city to bomb. This graffiti success provided AME with an opportunity to get an education. He had heard about writers going to art school, and he decided that was his only shot.

I was expected to go to college. My mom teaches French and Latin. In high school I was smart, but I didn't have any grades except for the A's I would get in art classes. So I put together a portfolio of graffiti stuff and showed it to the folks at the [School of Visual Arts], and they were like, "You're in." When I visited, this kid who writes HAPPY took me around, and I saw VERT and other writer's tags up and I knew I would have something in common with the people there. At first I did graphic design because I thought I could make a little money and be an artist, but I found out quick that I couldn't do that. I'm going all the way, I want to be an artist, so I transferred into the Fine Art Department, but I'm not sure yet exactly what I want to do in painting, I'm still developing my own language. I guess I'm disillusioned by graffiti right now because it's such a confusing thing. It's only what you make of it. Graffiti applies to a lot of things in life, it's like a microcosm of

society. Every different type of character out there in society is also involved in graffiti. At first you think to yourself that every other graffiti
writer is gonna understand and be cool with you, but it's the total opposite. So many people are on a power trip, they're selfish, they think
"graffiti's all about me," and even if they know that it's not all about
them, they want it to be about them, so they do everything in their
power to make it about them. There are a lot of kids that know that
they're not that talented, but they don't care, they know they're bigger
than you and they'll kick your ass, and that's what they use.

I first met AME through VERT in November 1995, at the very beginning of this project. We were waiting outside of the club S.O.B.'s on the
West Side of Manhattan, and AME rolled up to say "hi," prior to embarking on his nightly painting mission. I didn't know many active writers at
that point, and I was excited when VERT introduced him. Full of youthful
enthusiasm, AME swung his messenger bag around and said, "You wanna
buy some paint? I'm a kleptomaniac and I got enough paint for a year, so I
might as well try and make some money. It's easier to rack in the suburbs,
and you can practice and get good. Rackin' in the city's hard." He soon left
to complete his mission, and I didn't see him again for almost a year, but
our relationship continued.

Two days later I was on the First Avenue platform waiting for the
L train and I came across an AME tag that caught my attention. He had
used a gold paint pen (most writers use silver), and his letters were un-
connected and equidistant across the top of an advertisement for a movie.
AME had very carefully placed his tag, stylizing both the letters and the
spaces between them. This made the tag easy to read while allowing him
to claim a larger amount of space than if the letters were connected.

Now that AME's tag was burned into my mind, I started to see it all over
the city. AME was very active on the streets for a good six- to eight-month
period, and I followed my own AME story all over New York. The yellow
throw-ups lining the tracks in the Bronx; the lone upside down "A," high up
the side of a building on Canal and Broadway in Manhattan; the fifteen red
and white throw-ups viewable from the Number 2 subway as it travels above
ground from 116th to 125th in Harlem; the throw-ups flanking the F train
way out in Coney Island; and the tags on mailboxes everywhere in Manhattan. With each throw-up and tag I saw, I got to know AME a little more.

Eight months later, in October 1996, I met AME again in person at
the Graffiti Symposium held at the Museum of the City of New York on

AME throw-up, SoHo.

Manhattan's Upper East Side. Because I had had such a close relationship to his work, and because he had become more famous as a writer, it was strange to meet again. AME was quiet and I didn't know if he remembered me, but he wound up in the seat next to me.

The keynote address was given by NYU professor Tricia Rose, author of *Black Noise: Rap Music and Black Culture in Contemporary America*. AME broke the ice by criticizing her economic formula for the rise of graffiti. "Too narrow," he said. At the end of her talk she announced that the New York Commissioner of Parks had shown up and demanded a slot on the podium. As the commissioner droned on about his success cleaning up graffiti in the city's parks, AME leaned over to me and said, "Graff is like a smoke alarm, when it goes off you don't throw away the smoke alarm, you check to see where the fire is." I thought this was interesting and thoughtful, so I asked him to do a word in my blackbook and he agreed.

Blackbook Interview

AME's messenger bag made a familiar metallic sound as he took it off his shoulder and lay it on the floor of my apartment with a clank. Contents: ten cans of spray paint; one hardcover book, *The Naked Ape* by Desmond Morris, the English anthropologist who writes on human behavior and evolution; and my blackbook, which he passed to me in silence. I looked

AME rooftop piece, Brooklyn.

with awe at the work and quickly got him seated for an interview. First, I asked him why he chose the pages for "family" and "quality of life" in the blackbook.

> I always have dreams about my family and it's what's had the biggest effect on my life. My family situation is what kept me writing. I didn't really write so much for other writers. I wrote just for the mission, just to get out of the house and get my mind on something else. This piece shows that it's not all bad, though. It's effected me in positive and negative ways.
>
> With this second piece I just went more towards the life thing than the quality. "Quality of Life" is just a category of misdemeanors that the mayor made up to get rid of shit he didn't like. I was thinking more about life and reproduction.

Since I had seen so much of AME's work in the streets, I turned the discussion back to bombing, which on the surface appears merely as a quest for fame. I remembered putting my own tag up and worrying about what people would think of me and my horrible tag. However, putting yourself in public for others to judge can have positive side effects. Repetitive name painting on public surfaces can play a crucial role in a writer's development of a critical awareness. AME discussed how his experience bombing had an important impact on his development as an artist and as a person.

AME, illustration of the page for "Family" from the author's blackbook.

You need to find a balance between not caring at all what people think and caring too much. Sometimes you're just like, "I'm doing what I want, I don't care," and then other times you look at shit and be like, "Why did I do that? People must think I'm an idiot." So bombing makes you more thoughtful, and you can't get there without it, because it provides the critique. Bombing is like showing your portfolio, only it's not your whole portfolio, it's just a small portion of it. It's like a calling card. It says, "This is me and a hint of what I'm about. If you remember this and you're curious enough, maybe you'll pursue it more and find out the rest of the story."

I had been right to see AME's work as a mode of self-expression, but at the time I was not able to read the clues that helped to form a picture of the person behind the paint can. AME taught me about the subtleties of street graffiti, providing me with the tools needed to understand that in graffiti style, form follows function. The way a person writes on the streets tells a lot about who they are and what they want to accomplish with their graffiti.

You can tell what kind of person somebody is by where they paint or how their style is. You can tell if a guy is smaller if he climbs a lot to hit high spots. Because you know that a big dude ain't gonna be climbing all over the place. Those dudes are generally just on the ground because they have no reason to climb. Smaller dudes generally climb a lot because they want to avoid confrontation and write on clean space rather than over other writers.

My throw-up isn't your typical bubbly, bomber's throw-up style. It's more like a straight-letter style, so the proportions are really important. I like my throw-up to look like letters rather than a bubbly throw-up, which is a more abstract representation. I was never a really heavy street bomber at first, though I did my share. I started off bombing on highways where you can take more time. So my throw-up wasn't really designed for speed, it was designed for clarity, to be readable, so you'd remember it.

AME isn't interested only in individual graffiti writers, but in the culture as a whole. He says piecing style tells us about the expression of one individual, whereas a bombed wall reveals the interactions between different writers, and AME likes to decipher the story embedded in the wall. AME's appreciation for the stories that bombing reveals makes him a bit opinionated when it comes to legal walls and elaborate styles. He says he likes to look at tags and throw-ups more than pieces. He thinks

AME, illustration of the page for "Quality of Life" from the author's blackbook.

that some writers are stuck in a rut of imitation and just aren't being that original.

A legal wall to do graffiti is a place where you have a chance to really, really do your shit. If you have the time to do it and really put some thought into it, I think you should do something that's really different. It seems like a lot of guys do legal walls just to get their ups, but they're gettin' their ups in a legal way. They just accumulate legal walls, but they're not giving anything back to the viewer, except for another fancy piece, and I think the days of fancy pieces are over.

Anybody can get a legal wall. It doesn't matter, you don't even have to show your own work, you can bring in flicks of [a better-known writer.] It used to be when I first started seeing guys do legal walls I was like, "That guy's good, he got a legal wall, he must've earned it." But that's not the case. There is a lot of conning of stupid, ignorant, businessmen that goes on.

Finally I ask AME what he means by saying that graff is like a smoke alarm.

Graffiti is trying to say a lot of things. First it says, "Who are you to own this?" Second, every graffiti writer wants some amount of attention. It's pretty immature to write your name on a wall and be like, "Look at me, look at me," but there are some that don't want to exist on that level, hopefully you grow out of that. Graffiti is trying to say something deeper. We're in such a huge city and so many people are making all these changes and there's all this shit going on, like all these advertisements and all this shit being thrown at you, and it's kinda like, "What about me? I'm somebody too." And then when you write graffiti you're like, "Yeah, I am somebody, and everyone's gonna know that I'm somebody, that I'm alive and that I'm around." It's like self-promotion. You go out and promote yourself because no one else is. Graffiti is a signal that the youth of the city are not being noticed. Constantly they're taking money out of schools, destroying art programs, and a lot of graffiti writers are the kids that the schools did not nurture or guide, so they went out on their own and said, "Fuck you, I'm being treated like I'm nobody and now I'm somebody." The Vandal Squad just tries to arrest children. I think they need to think more about why these kids are doing this. It's not just acceptance from your peers. There are certain kids who write just for the kids in the neigh-borhood, but it goes deeper than that. They should give these kids something to really feel proud of.

AME then tells me about a dream he had:

> I dreamt that I was being chased by leopards. I couldn't physically out-run them so I climbed a tree, thinking I was smarter. Then the leop-ards started to climb the trees also, so then I used the only advantage I had, I woke up. I knew that I could just leave 'em, so I did.

Because AME has slowed down a little and taken himself off of the front lines, he has been able to develop an understanding with himself. He no longer needs the fix that graffiti once provided. Maybe he's also real-ized that the leopards are getting a little too close, and therefore it's time to try something different.

ΛΝΛΖΣ

Out-of-Towner Gets Up in the Tunnel

I first started seeing AMAZE mop tags in thick black ink in the winter of 1995. I was also seeing a lot of TWIST tags at the time, and their similarity made me think that TWIST was commenting on his own work: TWIST AMAZES. "Does TWIST sometimes write AMAZE?" I asked NAVEL one night at McGovern's.

"No, that's his boy."

In the spring of 1997 I noticed a new AMAZE tag on the dumpster outside the bodega in my neighborhood. Two days later I was speaking to KAWS on the phone. "AMAZE is in town," he said.

"I know," I said.

That night I met AMAZE, a twenty-one-year-old white kid from San Francisco. His usual gear consists of white t-shirt and Dickie work pants, with black synthetic leather shoes. AMAZE is a straight-edge vegan, which means no alcohol and no animal products. He is of Irish descent and wears his claddagh ring proudly.[1] He is six-foot-two, skinny, has long arms and dark hair. He flashed a humble smile of genuine surprise when I let on that I was aware of his exploits as a writer. He is famous.

In San Francisco AMAZE works hard at his graffiti. "I paint an average of seven fill-ins a week. I haven't been painting that long," said AMAZE, who started when he was 18, "but I paint a lot, so I've gotten good fast, plus I've been lucky to have some great teachers like TWIST and KR." AMAZE was also a math major at San Francisco City University.

I called AMAZE the next day to paint on my roof. He didn't have any paint but said that he'd like to come over and check the spot. He came over around 3:15 and we went up to the roof of my building. "I think I'll be able to pull something off," he said, and we went back down to my apartment. I showed him my blackbook and he went through it slowly. "Do you want to do a word?" I asked.

"No," he said.

"You haven't yet mastered the alphabet."

"Not well enough to do a piece in a blackbook that a lot of writers are going to see."

He continued to page through the book and chuckled when he noticed that the words "white" and "power" came after each other. He slid one page up jokingly so it said "white power." "Go ahead do that," I encouraged him, eager to broach the topic of race. AMAZE asked for a Paper Mate medium-point ballpoint pen, but I could only offer my Pilot Precise Rolling Ball.

AMAZE began to draw as I peppered him with questions about race and graffiti. He wasn't prepared for this level of discussion and became reticent.

> GS: "What's it like to be a white graffiti writer?"
> AMAZE: "I don't know."
> GS: "Well, the public perception in New York is that many writers are . . . black."
> AMAZE: "Yeah, it's the same in SF."
> GS: "Can you name many active black writers?"
> AMAZE: "DOM. ADER. Nope, not that many."

Despite the fact that he chose to write on a page that said "white power," AMAZE was not interested in getting into a discussion about race. He was trying to be funny and ironic. I was disappointed that I failed to engage AMAZE in *my* political debate, but he remained good natured. On the page he did an "AMAZE" outline and wrote the slogan "Fly Ass White Boy" next to it.

Happy Easter

On the night of Easter Sunday I ran into AMAZE at McGovern's. AMAZE doesn't drink and he quickly got bored at the bar. "Let's go," he said, "I wanna catch some tags." We were both on bicycles and we toured SoHo, stopping frequently for AMAZE to tag a mailbox or a door. AMAZE's bombing kit this night consisted of a "mop," which is an emptied black shoe polish bottle filled with thick black ink. His second shoe polish bottle was filled with silver ink made out of a substance he called the "secret sauce." In the highly competitive atmosphere of graffiti, writers are very secretive with their techniques and supplies, but AMAZE finally revealed the substance was KRink, a specialized ink created by graffiti writer KR.[2] He also carried a small silver paint pen for out-of-the-way spots.

AMAZE tagged SoHo heavily, but the ease of catching tags with his "mop," which is significantly quieter than aerosol, decreased the risk and for me made it almost boring. But it's all work and no play for AMAZE. He would take his marker out of his messenger bag and tag the door and get back on his bike, no noise, no smell, no nonsense, just a lot of drips that showed on his pants all too well.

SoHo is a Mecca for out-of-state writers, and AMAZE recognized tags from San Francisco, Los Angeles, and Ohio. Most out-of-town writers, like most tourists, tend to stay in Manhattan unless they have a guide to the outer "inner city" boroughs. AMAZE's ink was running dry so we ended our night of tagging; we were out for two hours.

The next time I saw AMAZE he was wearing a brand new Columbia University sweater. "I was beginning to get discouraged," he said. "It's tough to rack here in New York, because there is so much security. Then I was at the Columbia bookstore and I got myself socks, boxers, and this sweater." Just the necessities, I guess. AMAZE was in a good mood and continued to update me on his exploits. "You know that parking lot on Crosby Street you took me to with all the pieces? I got bored today so I went and did a little JOSH piece in there."

"In broad daylight you pulled off a piece," I asked, a little skeptical.

"Yeah, I did the whole thing in like fifteen minutes. This guy came over like, 'What are you doing?' I said, 'Graffiti,' and he said he was calling the cops. So I just finished up and walked off."

AMAZE returned to San Francisco to take his final exams, but I continued to see his tags. Months passed. Then one day in early summer I did a doubletake on an AMAZE tag that I hadn't seen before. That night AMAZE showed up at the vegan organic restaurant where I work to get some food. He was in New York to spend his summer vacation.

Rooftop Fireworks

ESPO and AMAZE developed a strong working relationship over the course of the summer that began with a legal rooftop in Harlem. Then after a few trial missions they landed a second rooftop that can be seen by everyone crossing the Manhattan Bridge. This illegal piece required a huge ladder, which the duo purchased at a considerable discount. ESPO recounted the story.

One night, around the first of July, we climbed an easily accessible fire escape to the roof. We did some throw-ups. AMAZE came off in a good spot. My shit was butt. I saw the spot we eventually got and told AMAZE, "We're getting that spot and I'm getting the left side so I can come off on the street as well as from the bridge." We walked through an open door on the roof, through the building, and discovered, at 4:30 A.M., that the front door was open.

On July 4th we went to Home Depot, which, God Bless America, was open. We got paint, rollers, and the ladder for about ninety dollars. We arrived at the roof at 5:00 P.M. and got started. The cops yelled at us at about 6:00 P.M., but we stayed and painted, ignoring the fireworks, till about 1:00 A.M. Then we packed up and went home.

However, neither man could sleep that night as visions of their wall kept the adrenaline in their systems. At 6:45 A.M. AMAZE called ESPO, who picked up on the first ring. "Let's go," AMAZE said.

The front door of the building had a broken lock, so this time they took the stairs to the roof. Both men were exhausted and one would sleep while the other painted. During the afternoon a resident of the building took a liking to their work and invited them to have a barbecue up there sometime. They finally finished early in the evening on Saturday.

ESPO called as soon as they were finished. I immediately left my house to check it out but was unable to find it on my own. Later that night, as we were riding home, AMAZE asked hesitantly, "You wanna check out the rooftop?" We pedaled through the sleepy Chinatown streets, periodically catching tags with a can of red Rustoleum. AMAZE had his can out, ready to make his mark on a white wall with sparse tags, when I noticed a cop car slowly patrolling the streets. "Five-O," I whispered, and he slid his can back into his bag and popped the quick-release on the front tire of his bicycle. He looked hard at his wheel, trying to determine the mysterious problem as the police drove past us without event. "Bombing on bikes is the shit," exclaimed AMAZE.

The Tunnel Revisited

A few weeks later AMAZE was sitting at my kitchen table looking through graffiti mags and drawing his name on a piece of scrap paper. He turned the page over and began to read my early draft of the chapter "The

ESPO, 1995

STRUGGLE

Tunnel." "You went to the FREEDOM tunnels?" he asked. "Could you take me there?" His voice had changed in tone from boredom to excitement.

"Sure," I responded, "we can go tomorrow." I hadn't been to the tunnel since June 30, 1996, two days before Amtrak's "Safety Improvement Project" required them to put up "security enhancements." "I'm not sure if we can get in, but I can at least show you the graffiti on the surrounding walls."

The next afternoon around 3:00 I met AMAZE at his place. "Do you mind if we make a quick stop at the bicycle shop?" he asked, still trying to wake up. "I need to rack a bag for ESPO."

"I don't mind, but I'll wait down the street if that's OK," I responded. AMAZE is an accomplished shoplifter, but I knew that my nerves would get us both caught. AMAZE gave me the paint in his bag to make room for a new one and I walked down the street to wait for him. In less than five minutes we were walking casually toward the subway. I shot AMAZE a questioning glance and he returned it with an affirmative nod. On the platform waiting for the uptown F train AMAZE unfolded a seventy-five-dollar messenger bag. I thought this was an impressive feat, but AMAZE was unfazed by his heist. On the train he told me stories of some of his best heists and scams. Mostly he only steals graffiti supplies and bike parts. "I like graffiti, bikes, and racking," he said. However, he wouldn't tell me his secret New York paint racking spot. We exited the train in good spirits and headed for the tunnel.

The entrance to the tunnel was closed off by an imposing fence, but the absence of razor wire made it easy to climb over. In the tunnel, the damp, still air and the serene quiet quickly consumed us, providing a clean break from the bright sunny day of a minute ago. AMAZE walked ahead of me, excited about the graffiti and the solitude of the tunnel. "This is cool," he shouted back to me.

"There used to be homes down here," I said. "They've all been destroyed." There was a conspicuous lack of graffiti on the walls where homes used to be—only nails that now held no picture frames. The tunnel was quiet and lonely, and the silence spoke of a longing for its former inhabitants.

A shiny new sturdy steel fence about ten feet high ran along the side of the tracks, preventing us from getting close to the graffiti on the east wall. But after five minutes of walking the fence stopped abruptly. Either Amtrak had yet to complete its work or they were severely underestimating the will of the folks who spend time in the tunnel. AMAZE couldn't hold back any longer. The first chance he got he headed straight for the east wall. "Here's a good spot," he said. It was under a grate and fairly well lit. "Everyone who comes down here from now on is gonna see this." He pulled cans from his bag and peered at them, trying to discern their color.

I had told AMAZE that the walls of the tunnel were very porous because of the moisture and would require a lot of paint. AMAZE solved this problem by going over a poorly done piece from a writer neither of us knew. AMAZE got busy quickly, putting his outline on the wall. Then he slowed down realizing the tunnel was secure. "I'm gonna take my time with this," he said, relishing the opportunity.

I sat down on the tracks and watched, taken in by the rhythmic blasts of the paint can. This was my third trip to the tunnel and I felt comfortable. AMAZE worked hard on his piece, channeling all of his energy into the wall. As the smell of aerosol started to win out over the dank smell of the tunnel, AMAZE's piece began to take shape. He challenged himself creatively by painting a letter style that he hadn't attempted before, and I could tell he was pleased.

We walked deeper into the tunnel and the light grew dim, so I took out my flashlight. To the people who used to live in the tunnel a flashlight was a symbol of authority, and anyone venturing into the dark with a light was dealt with accordingly. Now that no one lived down here it was safe to have a light. We walked to ESPO's Unabomber and AMAZE photographed it as well as the black-and-white character done by TWIST. AMAZE caught some tags on the wall near his friend's work and we proceeded deeper into the tunnel.

We came to another area where light pours in from some high arching grates, and AMAZE took the opportunity to do a small piece with his

AMAZE, Freedom Tunnel, August, 1997.

TWIST (with VERT and GWIZ tags, upper left), Freedom Tunnel, August 1997.

leftover paint. This piece didn't "come off," he said, and now that AMAZE was completely out of paint our mission became one of exploration and appreciation.

Next we came to the spot where VERT and I had come last summer, the day before Amtrak destroyed the homes of the inhabitants. VERT did a simple piece on the west wall, and I wrote a simple poem on the east wall in colored chalk and paint.

We walked a little further and explored the area in the cement embankment where Bernard and his friends once had their homes. Now there was only rubble. Where once a barbecue pit had been a testament to man's adaptive strength, now rotting boards showed the strength of a corporation to look past its own humanity. In what used to be the living room was a large rendering of Goya's *Third of May* done by FREEDOM and SMITH.

AMAZE was impressed with all the art the tunnel had to offer. "Thanks for bringing me down here," he said. "I'm glad I got to come down here before I left. I've heard a lot about this place. Hey, I got a spot I wanna do a small piece at. Do you want to come and look out for me?"

"Sure," I said not knowing fully what my job would be.

Above Ground

I showed up at AMAZE's crib about 12:30 A.M. His apartment was in a state of boxed transition; he was moving out and others were preparing to move in. AMAZE sat calmly on the bed doing a piece in a blackbook belonging to SMK, a writer from Washington, D.C. After he finished we paged through the book together and discussed the pieces we liked by ESPO, MEK, and CLARK–FLY ID. AMAZE's favorite was by SEIN 5.

We had been relaxing for about an hour with no mention of going out to paint and none of the nervous energy that I assumed would be normal prior to a painting an illegal piece. "I guess I'm gonna go home," I said, as I was getting tired. AMAZE was surprised.

"You're not gonna come with me to do this spot?"

"I thought that you'd given up on it."

"Hell no."

AMAZE got up and started rummaging around his apartment looking for two socks. He had on a white t-shirt but didn't change into bombing gear. Lots of writers like to wear black and pull a baseball cap down over their faces to look inconspicuous, but AMAZE wore what he had on. Then he started rattling around under his sink to find enough paint to do the job. "I guess I can use this blackberry (Krylon) for the fill, but I don't know how it'll turn out, I've never used it before," said AMAZE apologetically. He put the cans in his bag for the second time today, and off we went.

On the way to the spot I asked what he expected me to do. "If you see anybody who looks like they'd call the cops, whistle. As far as the cars go, only whistle if a cop stops at the light."

The spot AMAZE had chosen was a parking lot at the corner of Lafayette and Spring streets in Manhattan, across the street from a fire station, two doors up from the bike store he had racked from earlier in the day. This was a good spot because he was fairly well hidden behind some cars and couldn't easily be seen from the street. It was a relatively low-risk endeavor for AMAZE. Only the faint smell of aerosol and the clack-clack of the ball-bearing rattling in the metal might give him away. He had four colors to do fill-in, outline, 3-D, and an outline around everything. He started painting at 1:46 A.M., and twenty minutes later we stood admiring the fairly simple, straightforward letter design he had gotten up in a high-traffic area.

THE GRATE GRAFFITI SOLUTION

ESPO's Public Surface Announcement

On a snowy day in January 1997 ESPO called to update me on his latest assault—his first strike of this magnitude in Manhattan. In New York City, when a business closes for the night they seal their spot with metal roll-down grates that protect the windows and entrance. On Broadway at the corner of 12th Street, ESPO had used a brush to paint the four grates silver at 7:30 in the evening on a Friday. As folks walked by, they assumed that he was cleaning up the tags and the throw-ups on the silver grates.

The next day he returned with black to turn each of the approximately twelve-by-eight-foot grates into giant letters. In order to mask his real objective, he didn't go from right to left completing each letter—rather, he skipped around, painting a little bit here and there and trying to make it look abstract until the last possible moment, before making a quick exit.

This silver and black ESPO piece was twelve feet high and fifty feet long, with black filling out the small areas of negative space, turning each grate into a letter. COST and REVS were among the first writers to use bucket paint in the service of graffiti. In ESPO's case, using bucket paint to paint over old tags and throw-ups distanced him from the graffiti subculture. In the larger society and in the media, aerosol paint is connected to graffiti vandalism. ESPO instead appeared to the public to be an anti-graffiti vigilante.

ESPO's work was a self-serving act of public service. He was taking the initiative to cover up some of the worn-out tags and fill-ins in the area and giving them new life with his own kind of buff. He appeared to be performing a service to the neighborhood, but he was also taking over whole city blocks with his name. This work highlighted the space between the entrenched polarities of graffiti. It was part graffiti clean-up, part graffiti art. ESPO was doing illegal work without permission that generated appreciation from the property owners. He was covering up the faded tags with

ESPO, 12th and Broadway. Photograph © S. Powers: courtesy of the artist.

a new form of name painting that the public had a hard time discerning as graffiti. He didn't use the spray paint, bold colors, or complicated letter styles associated with a despised subculture. ESPO's giant pieces actually deflected attention more than they commanded it.

Almost a month to the day later, ESPO was out on the streets "cleaning up" the graffiti. On a mild winter afternoon he was on the corner of 6th Avenue and Canal Street nonchalantly using his brush and roller to paint over all of the graffiti on the seven roll-down grates of an abandoned store. This spot has heavy car traffic, but no one thought he was doing anything illegal. One concerned citizen even stopped to swap graffiti clean-up stories and to give him advice on how to best cover it up.

Two days later ESPO returned to the spot to put the signature on his graffiti solution. With a few strokes of his black paint brush he turned the freshly painted silver grates into a giant ESPO piece with at least nine cops in full view.

This was risky, but he had two things in his favor: Not many people could see that he was doing graffiti because of the common perception that it's only graffiti if you use aerosol and write your name in a typically expected style. This narrow view leaves a lot of room for writers who are willing to expand their horizons. The second side of Steve's double-edged sword was that his technique was more pleasing to the eyes of the general public, who have been taught to associate graffiti names with crime and violence.

This two-sidedness to all of ESPO's work is at the heart of his unselfishness as an artist. His painting does not intrude or force itself upon you. If you don't make the effort to notice it, his work ignores you. If you do notice, however, ESPO rewards in ways you never thought possible with graffiti.

The saga of ESPO's "grate graffiti solution" continued to expand its reach over the graff populace while playing with public perception. His third effort at restoring the faith of graffiti took place at 125th Street and Malcolm X Boulevard in Harlem. Again ESPO painted huge silver and black letters. Some Harlem writers took umbrage at having their names painted over but knew that they didn't have an argument because they couldn't compete with ESPO's originality and creativity. However, ESPO is more than willing—sometimes too willing—to back up his work physically, if the situation presents itself.

In the beginning of the summer ESPO took his graffiti solution to Jerome Avenue in the Bronx. After four days of dragging his ladder on the subway he finally finished his largest grate piece to date, Utilizing two grates for each letter, it was 15 feet high and almost 120 feet long. Often writers will put up other writers' names along with their own as a sign of respect, and sometimes of gratitude. This piece was dedicated to four veteran Bronx writers who noted and appreciated other grates he did: "4 COPE, CHAD, YOGI, LOUIE." Some younger Bronx writers were less

ESPO, Jerome Avenue, Bronx. Photograph © S. Powers: courtesy of the artist.

than hospitable to this piece and saw it as a good way to get fame, so they tagged over it. ESPO fixed his piece later that summer and then had Bronx legend COPE keep an eye on it for him.

Just before Christmas ESPO lit up my answering machine. "It's Steve. Check out the West Side Highway and 39th Street when you get a chance," chirped the message. I walked to the spot the next morning and was overwhelmed by the magnitude of the piece. Steve painted "ESPO!" on five grates covering 150 feet in length and reaching 20 feet high. It was just huge. This spot took three long days to complete, and while he was painting the owner of the building came out. "What's this gonna cost me?" the owner asked. "Nothing," ESPO replied. "I just got sick of looking at it the way it was." ESPO let him know he was going to add some personal touches but the owner didn't care either way.

On January 3, 1998, almost a year to the day since his first grate initiative, ESPO left a message informing me of two new spots: one in Brooklyn, on the corner of Court Street and Schermerhorn, with REVS; the other by himself on the Bowery, next to CBGB's. For these spots ESPO used red and white. That night ESPO and I talked about his work for a long time on the phone. In Brooklyn, people asked why he was painting the grates. "I just got sick of looking at it the way it was," he would reply, sounding like an anti-graffiti community activist.

A few days later I learn that he had painted his name on four grates in Queens overlooking the Queensboro Bridge. He told me that while he was painting the owners of the restaurant next door noticed him and asked, "When are you gonna paint our grates?"

"When are you closed?" replied ESPO a little taken a back.

"Saturday." ESPO told me that he planned on passing the spot on to REVS.

This group of letters had a white fill-in and red "3-D." From the street the piece boomed, but when you got on the train to return to Manhattan it really revealed itself. It's always about context, and in this case ESPO had taken on all Queens comers to Manhattan. ESPO's piece was on the street, but the rooftop of the building was riddled with throw-ups and tags from some of Queens's best writers. From the window of the elevated train both ESPO's grate solution and more traditional graffiti now competed for attention.

Three days later, ESPO called to say that he painted his name on grates in Staten Island, his fourth piece of the year. "All City," I congratulated him, but ESPO wasn't yet ready to accept the title.

ESPO, West Side Highway and 39th St. Photograph © Steve Powers.

"Now I gotta get up in Corona, Brownsville, and East New York," ESPO said, referring to some of the city's more famous forgotten neighborhoods. "REVS says that I gotta do about a dozen more, and I'm going by that."

Good luck, I thought, not wanting to doubt ESPO's resolve. By March, ESPO had completed twenty-seven grates. "The conversation I'm having with the city," he said, "just continues to evolve."

By 1999 ESPO was no longer promoting himself simply as an individual intent on doing good works, but rather as a member of a community-based activist group. "ESPO" became an acronym for Exterior Surface Painting Outreach, "a volunteer organization dedicated to making the world a different place." ESPO provided a community service by cleaning up graffiti-weary grates and then branded each grate with its logo so that the public would know who was responsible for these good works.

In July 1999 St. Martin's Press published ESPO's book *The Art of Getting Over: Graffiti at the Millennium* by Stephen Powers. At this point ESPO claimed more than seventy grates cleaned and beautified, but he laid down his buckets and brushes when he began to notice a surveillance van parked on his block. Steve Powers also began the process of shedding his ESPO alter-ego and making a name for himself as an author and artist.

In August 1999 He allowed himself to be photographed (in disguise) and interviewed by Nina Siegel for the *New York Times*. He spoke openly about his method and insisted that he was providing a positive public service. "The neighborhood gets the benefit of my cleaning it up and I get my name up there," Powers said. "I'm a real product of the Giuliani era."[1]

If the anti-graffiti forces had been unaware that ESPO was a graffiti writer, this article served notice. The surveillance also increased as the vandal squad was now starting to understand that ESPO posed a threat because he proved to the public that graffiti writers could be positive, proactive members of the community and that not all graffiti is vandalism.

On a Monday in late November, ESPO told the listeners of WLIB radio that he was painting a portrait of Mayor Giuliani and that they should come down to Washington Square Park the next day and pay a dollar for the privilege of throwing fake dung at it. This stunt, concocted by artist Joey Skaggs, was an effort to get back at the mayor for his attempt to shut down the Brooklyn Museum's show *Sensations*, which featured a painting of the Madonna with elephant dung. Giuliani tried to cut off the museum's funds because he declared the art offensive to Christians; however, the Brooklyn Museum filed a successful lawsuit against the mayor's attempt at censorship and the show was kept open, with the city required to resume funding.

The next day, six vandal squad detectives came to Steve's door and announced that he was under arrest. They said that he had been the subject of an ongoing investigation, and they confiscated enough of his personal belongings to fill five garbage bags, including the contents of his hard drive, the film *American Graffiti*, and a pair of brass knuckles that were hanging decoratively in his kitchen. For this last item Powers was charged with possession of a weapon, as well as six counts of graffiti felony. (The weapons charge was eventually dropped.)

The police response to ESPO's public high jinks was also in part fueled by his satiric account of them in his book. During his arrest the cops told Steve that they were not amused by his account of vandal cops as semismart, stressed-out, overweight men who secretly desired fame as much as the writers they pursued.[2]

Powers treatment at the hands of the police generated sympathetic press coverage in the *Village Voice*.[3] His treatment by the courts, however, was serious. With the assistance of progressive lawyer Ron Kuby, Powers battled for the return of his personal items and fought the case against him. None of the property owners would file a complaint against ESPO, and he finally pled down to two counts of criminal mischief and served five days of community service.

This tangle with the police effectively ended ESPO's career as a graffiti writer, and he began to focus more attention on his studio work. In 2000 he was involved in a group showed called *Indelible Market* at the Institute of Contemporary Art in Philadelphia. Later this show also traveled to New York, and then to the Venice and Liverpool biennials, which showcase emerging artists. Most recently Steve has teamed up with the public art organization Creative Time to curate the repainting and revitalization of the signs at Coney Island.

Today Steve is serious about art but still has a sense of humor about himself.

My achievements thus far have been the result of selling a style that is a good mix of intelligence, humor, and attitude. I've talked about brand building and positioning, and I'm also aware of the cycles that cause brands to lose appeal. So now the emphasis is on creating a body of work that shows constant growth so people get into it for the long haul. Right now is possibly the moment where people who are ready to emerge as artists, who can contribute to the history of painting, are going to be given that opportunity. Critics and curators are ready to give a few artists the keys to the art world, so they can pump new energy into the field. Barry McGee could probably do it single-handed, but there's room for a school to come into session. There are many more artists that can see the opportunity but are just slinging some overwrought graffiti style and hoping the energy of the movement will get them paid too. I don't care about the financial aspects, I want to make durable work that speaks to the time and the people in it—their hopes and frustrations at not realizing those hopes. I take art as a serious responsibility.[4]

3

GETTING OUT

OVER THE WALL

Graffiti Media and Creating a Career

*C*an writing graffiti lead to a career? In this final part of the book, I depart from the ethnographic observations that have been central to this work thus far and focus more squarely on the notion of "subculture." As previously suggested, much of the scholarship on subcultures suggests that participation in such worlds is, in effect, a dead end. But I want to suggest that this is not the case here. Graffiti writers can create a career path out of their subculture experiences, often using their writing as a springboard for other related career paths.

When graffiti murals graced the outside of New York city subway cars, from the early 1970s to the late 1980s, this controversial form of painting was not about making a career for oneself, but began as simple name-based "tags" or signatures done with magic marker. These quickly evolved into complex aerosol murals, which writers called masterpieces, or "pieces" for short. A writer's reputation became based on the frequency and the style of "getting up," which in turn produced the desired subcultural fame. While this movement drew the interest of teenagers, gallery owners, journalists, filmmakers, photographers, and artists, it drew the ire of public officials and some members of the community.

New York City mayors declared two separate wars on graffiti-writing urban teens, as discussed earlier, insisting that such writing constituted harmful vandalism and created a context for crime. They utilized the "broken windows" model introduced by Wilson and Kelling to argue that graffiti, not poverty, created an environment for subway crime. By the late 1980s the increase in graffiti arrests and the fortress-like fencing around the lay-ups had severely decreased painting on New York City subways, but by this time significant writing movements had been established in other parts of the country and the world.

The New York City train era came to a close in 1989, when the Metropolitan Transit Authority (MTA) refused to put painted trains into service. The subways could no longer be used as a medium of communication. Writers stopped painting exclusively on trains because they could no longer serve as a means to broadcast their deeds to the rest of the world. Without the potential for fame, the subways were no longer worth the risk.

Although writers quickly began to paint on walls all over the city, there were no longer central locations, like the so-called Writers Bench at the 149th Street and Grand Concourse subway station, where writers could view passing graffiti on the subways. The movement found a new medium for producing fame: the photograph. Photographs made ephemeral graffiti pieces permanent, allowing writers to view the work of others without attachment to a specific place or time. The inclusion of these "flicks" in magazines created a space where graffiti pieces from all over the world could come together to be judged, critiqued, and offered as instruction.[1]

For some writers, the mags are not simply documents of achievements but have become the new fame spot. Writers don't have to consider the potential audience of the actual spot; they paint, take a flick, and send it off to *12oz. Prophet, GSXL, On the Go, While You Were Sleeping,* or any other of the numerous graffiti magazines to be seen by thousands.[2] This has sped up the progression of the art form stylistically, but it has also produced a situation where regional distinctions are being wiped out and more and more pieces look the same. The ease of dissemination through the magazines has allowed more writers in isolated places to evolve into proficient graffiti artists quicker than would have been possible even a few years ago. But there is a blandness that accompanies this progress. As Steve Powers, editor, publisher, and writer of *On the Go,* noted in an interview, with globalization, regional differences become less distinct:

> Puerto Rico basically five years ago was painting very little. They would have dudes come down from New York or Philadelphia or wherever and they'd show some of the kids down there some shit, but it wasn't until they started getting *Can Control* [magazine] down there that their style started really progressing. Now you can see that these dudes can paint as well as anybody on a worldwide level. The only problem is that the whole dissemination of the culture is not leading people to be more creative. You got a lot of people who look like each other now. You got dudes in the Midwest who are doing pieces that look like Europe, and you got European pieces that obviously look

like New York. In some cities they got their own original style, and some cities are just copying New York. The problem is that people are getting the pictures without getting the full how to, they're getting the end result but they're not getting the process.

When writers began hitting subway trains in the early 1970s, the MTA was rather lax about cleaning the subway lines. Many of the early writers' pieces would run for as long as two years, and so work often wasn't photographed. As graffiti legend PHASE 2 recalls, "Assuming the pieces would always run, taking photos was not a widespread practice. . . . Picture-taking became more widespread when the transit [system] began to systematically clean pieces off trains somewhere around '74."[3] As pieces ran for shorter and shorter durations, flicks became the only way to record (and boast of) one's feats. Photos also became a learning tool, allowing writers to scrutinize and study their own work as well as the work of others.

By the early 1980s, with writers being treated like stars by some art galleries and members of the press, documentation of the graffiti subculture was undertaken by sympathetic outsiders, many of whom became advocates for the art and the artists.[4] Henry Chalfant and Martha Cooper joined forces in 1984 to produce the book *Subway Art*, a photographic exploration of some of the very best graffiti art. In 1987 Chalfant collaborated with James Prigoff on the book *Spraycan Art*, which documented the achievements of writers in other cities in the United States and around the world. These books, along with the films *Wild Style* (1983) and *Style Wars* (1985), played a significant role in the dissemination of graffiti culture beyond New York.[5]

As photographic and publishing technology became more accessible, writers themselves began to document their subculture. This started with the simple trading of photos,[6] but it quickly evolved into magazines and videos.[7] This transition allowed writers to take control over the representation of their subculture, as well as to reap possible financial rewards.

The International Graffiti Times, On the Go, and Beyond

The *International Graffiti Times*, or *IGT* (now called *The International Get Hip Times*, or *TIGHT*) was the first graffiti magazine. Established in 1983 by legendary pioneer PHASE 2 and editor/graffiti-advocate David Schmidlapp, it broke the ground that inspired the next generation. Originally done in black-and-white in a fold-out, subway map format, *IGT* was one of the first instances where graffiti wasn't exclusively about public space.

The transition from trading flicks to making magazines created a forum for ideas and meant that writers had something to say as a community. This was a significant development in the culture, as it created a space for intellectualism and fostered group solidarity among kids who were often demonized by the larger society.

IGT incorporated a political and intellectual consciousness that inspired Steve Powers, a.k.a. ESPO, to start his own magazine. *On the Go* was founded in Philadelphia in 1989 as a response to the negative media campaign initiated by a group in Philadelphia called the Anti-Graffiti Network. Sociologist Howard Becker argues that those who maintain the forces of social control construct the behavior of outsiders as deviant and use this as an opportunity to enforce authority. He calls these folks "moral entrepreneurs," and anti-graffiti campaigns across the country have been politically and economically profitable to those "moral entrepreneurs" who engage in them.[8] Both Ferrell and Austin have shown in detail the ways that many anti-graffiti campaigns have less to do with the specifics of graffiti than with the political and economic goals of those who orchestrate them.[9] Played out in the media, these campaigns, which insist that graffiti is always vandalism and never art, did not go unnoticed by graffiti writers, who saw them as opportunistic and hypocritical—especially given the fact that artists, collectors, critics, journalists, and even some corporations were by now defining graffiti as a legitimate artistic pursuit—and one that, at times, could generate considerable money.

While Ferrell and Austin have established that political and economic opportunity often lie at the heart of anti-graffiti campaigns, few studies have analyzed how this construction of graffiti as an urban problem affects graffiti writers themselves.[10] Classic Chicago School criminology developed the idea of labeling theory to describe the process whereby deviance is socially constructed. Labeling theory advanced the notion that the forces of social control reinforce certain groups as outsiders by labeling their behaviors as deviant. Following labeling theory's model of secondary deviance, the affixing of a criminal label may further entrench those labeled in a life of criminality. However, rather than simply embarking on a self-fulfilling "life of crime," some graffiti writers chose legitimate means with which to counter their negative publicity. Writers responded by creating their own media to combat the perception that they were, in ESPO's words, "immoral idiots," and sought to offer magazines with mind-blowing art and thoughtful critical analyses. ESPO was well aware of the culture's need to have a voice of its own.

In Philly they basically sanitized the press. The Anti-Graffiti Network taught the press that they couldn't really show graffiti in a positive light anymore. I enjoyed some pretty good folk art style coverage in Philly in like '85 and '86, but by the time '87 rolled around it was all really negative articles and they were twisting and convoluting every-thing writers were saying. In Philly, the Anti-Graffiti Network had launched a P.R. campaign to make writers look stupid, and inconse-quential. They shut down any sign that writers were doing good things and were trying to do positive things until we came along. We in turn launched a counterattack to put writers on the map—to make writers look smart and show them in a little better light than they were at that moment.[11]

Inspired by *IGT*, and seeing the need for a positive media outlet, Pow-ers and his friends were also influenced by artists of the past who took it upon themselves to use their artistic talents to affect change. In his book *Lipstick Traces: A Secret History of the 20th Century*,[12] Greil Marcus traces a path from the German Dadaists to the French Situationists, and on to the English and later American punk scenes of the mid-1970s and 1980s. This book was widely read among youth with punk-rock proclivities, and for many it became an inspiring testament connecting them to a history that was previously untold. This secret history, however, was not exclusively the domain of white suburban punks and hardcore kids. Graffiti writers— some punks themselves, others not—were also influenced by the D.I.Y. (do-it-yourself) ethos of punks, whose little 'zines were getting people's attention.

Stephen Duncombe was one of the first in the academy to study these 'zines, and he argues in his book *Notes from Underground* that 'zines have a particular aesthetic formula in both design and content.[13] They are cheaply made, intentionally amateurish, and are usually the work of one individ-ual. Zinesters, as he calls them, are mostly suburban, white, middle-class kids, many of whom are punks and express an anarchistic spirit that makes them relish their outsider status.

Duncombe claims, though, that these types of 'zines are not exclusive to punk subculture, and he finds this style of publication across a broad range of subcultures, beginning with sci-fi fans in the late 1950s. His main argument is that 'zines in turn create a subculture of both readers and writers who find solace in an anonymous collectivity and the expression of middle-class ennui.

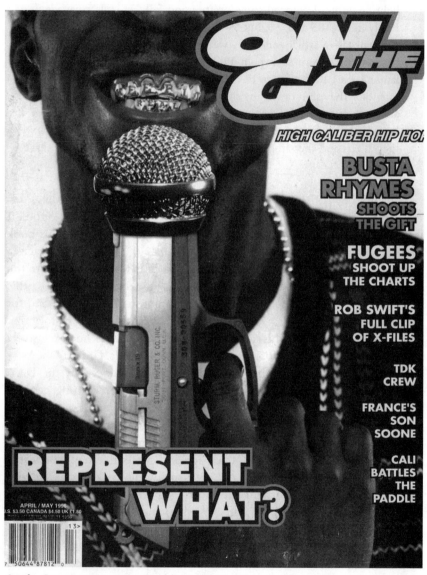

On the Go magazine cover, April/May 1996. Courtesy of Ari Forman, art director.

Chris Atton, in his book *Alternative Media*,[14] suggests that a commitment to political and social change is at the core of alternative media. His definition includes a focus not only on the content, but also on the collective activities involved in the production of alternative media, from researching and writing to making copies and finding outlets for distribution. He argues that through working together to put out alternative media the individuals feel a sense of collective power that is in the end political.

The subculture that Duncombe and Atton describe comes about through the process of making media; zinesters are not simply reporting on or documenting a subculture. Cultural studies scholar Paul Hodkinson uses the term "subculture media" to describe media produced by members of existing subcultures with the intent of serving the needs of that subculture.[15] The creation of such media often comes after the creation of the subcultural form, and in many ways it expands the reach of the subculture beyond geographic and physical space. While magazines such as *On the Go* and *While You Were Sleeping* share elements of attitude and process with 'zines, they are different in politics, style, and purpose. They do not create a subculture so much as document and disseminate it to other members. The form these media take will serve the needs of that subculture, so studying them can reveal the political and social implications of a specific subculture.

Graffiti is a visual medium, and in order to present artistic achievements to a wider audience, magazines must have good color and good design, rather than the low production value of 'zines. In this case the magazines are not simply a forum for like-minded people to talk among and about themselves; they are integral to the progression of the form, providing access to and evaluation of the best graffiti, unencumbered by geography. Moreover, such magazines and websites document illegal activity—but the documents of that activity are themselves not illegal. Magazines and websites take graffiti out of its physical context, and in so doing serve to decriminalize it; as reproduced in a magazine, it is difficult to tell if a piece has been painted illegally on the side of a church or legally on a sanctioned wall.

On the Go magazine interior, Issue #14 [undated]. Courtesy of Ari Forman, art director.

On the Go magazine cover, Issue #14 [undated]. Courtesy of Ari Forman, art director.

On the Go Moves to NYC

While the founders of *On the Go* were influenced by punk and some of the early 'zines, they eventually shaped their magazine according to the needs of their culture. In the beginning the *On the Go* crew produced the magazine for themselves and for fun, but in 1993 they combined their politics with a newfound entrepreneurial spirit. ESPO met DES, a talented graphic designer named Ari Forman, and together they decided to make a hip hop magazine for graffiti writers. Powers became the publisher and editor and Forman the art director. By expanding their reach to cover not only graffiti but music as well, they found a way to generate some money, which in turn professionalized *On the Go* and allowed it to reach a national and international audience.

The content of *On the Go* consisted of creatively written reviews of rap records, interviews with graffiti artists, numerous graffiti pictures, and social and political commentary. While *OTG* was funny and irreverent, it also had serious sections such as "Neighborhood Watch," which kept writers in the know about various police activities and tactics.

On the Go, along with magazines like *GSXL*, *Ego Trip*, and *Can Control*, revolutionized the graffiti magazine game; in the process, they laid down the formula for future writers. Without products to push, graffiti magazines couldn't make enough money to sustain the high standards of color and design required to adequately show off graffiti. Hip hop solved this, as graffiti writers turned sales directors, convincing advertisers and record executives of the economic potential of this underground culture. This move also helped underground hip hop, providing a space for budding music journalists. Again, it is important to note the cultural symbiosis. Graffiti writers, some of whom had been to art school and were talented graphic designers, were the ones best equipped to begin this wave of grassroots underground journalism, and to provide space for aspiring music critics; hip hop magazines of the late 1990s like *Stress*, *Blaze*, and *XXL* all had former graffiti writers on their staffs.

But it takes more than a single writer and graphic designer to put out such magazines; a music editor, a photo editor, and other writers and graphic designers are also needed, along with folks in sales and distribution, and others to answer telephones, set up interviews, find suppliers, and keep the accounts. Where 'zines are typically one-person operations, graffiti magazines require a collective effort from people with a variety of skills. However, the one common requirement for most all of those in the production of graffiti magazines is status as a current or former graffiti writer. These magazines report on illegal activities and often use illegal graffiti tactics to market themselves, all of which require the skills and interpersonal trust developed by graffiti writers. The *On The Go* crew were in fact famous for their marketing techniques, which included illegal stickering of their magazine covers in spots intended to target both readers and potential advertisers. These tactics caught the eye of corporations interested in "non-traditional" marketing techniques and inspired former graffiti writer DES, a.k.a. Ari Forman, to start On the Go Marketing with ex-writer KEST, a.k.a. Gabe Banner, as his first employee.[16] The production of magazines on a larger, more professional scale also has had the effect of providing jobs, and for some, careers, in the publishing industry.[17]

Even though this entrepreneurial turn allowed magazines to improve their design and expand their reach, the magazine business would soon succumb to the efficiency of the internet as a showcase for graffiti. It was never Powers's intent to make a living in the long term from *On the Go*, anyway; as he says, "the magazine game is hard, I really want to paint." In 1999 the funds that were barely keeping *On the Go* alive dried up and the magazine was discontinued—a fate that some of its competitors would also soon meet.

New graffiti magazines do continue to emerge; yet many of these self-made publishers have turned to the Internet to showcase graffiti writing. In this way, graffiti and hip hop music have once again split, as the sites are much cheaper to run and therefore are freed from the hip hop/music-related funds needed for the high costs of printing. The first graffiti site, Art Crimes (www.graffiti.org), now showcases graffiti photos from all over the world and offers links to hundreds of graffiti sites with photos and articles, as well as links to spray paint manufacturers and chat rooms with the latest news from the streets. These sites are forging closer and closer ties among a vast population of underground illegal artists, who continue the process of turning illegal fame into legitimate, if alternative, adult careers.

WRITING STYLE

It's Not What You Wear

Graffiti writers are part of a subculture with a rich history, a distinct language, and a unique set of forms (tags, pieces, etc.) beliefs, and practices. Unlike some other subculture groups—punks and hip-hoppers, most notably—they do not share a distinct style of dress or music. The graffiti subculture is made up of a vast collection of folks spanning a diversity of races, generations, classes, gender, sexualities, and nations who write their names illegally and legally on public space.

A subculture is a smaller cultural group that exists within a larger social world. How these groups form and what their existence means for the society in general is a subject of great debate among sociologists, criminologists, and scholars of cultural studies. While much work is being done to expand the definition of subculture,[1] there has yet to be an understanding of it that can account for a culture like graffiti, which can be a lifelong pursuit and possibly even lead to a career beyond the subculture. Most sociologists, and others who have sought to understand what participation in a subculture means for the larger society, have done so at the expense of understanding the lived experience of the participants. I believe that there are certain empirical factors that have yet to be acknowledged in the theorizing of subcultures and their role in the larger society. While more recent scholarship has begun to understand the diversity of subculture membership and the range of political affiliations and meanings that exist within subcultures, most scholars remain narrowly focused on spectacular cultures that center around a particular style of dress and music, thus excluding cultures like graffiti.

The history of subculture studies begins in the 1940s and 1950s, when the main concern was with deviant subcultures and the formation of street gangs. American sociologists like Albert Cohen and criminologists like Richard Cloward and Lloyd Ohlin theorized that subculture was a generalized attempt to solve the problems of a subordinate class position and the disintegration of various communities.[2] In the 1960s Howard Becker defined a deviant subculture as a collection of folks whose behaviors were "sufficiently strange" to be labeled as outsiders by those in the mainstream, which then further entrenched their disavowal of mainstream culture.[3]

The most influential group of scholars to address the problem of youth subculture were those who came to be known as the Birmingham School, who established the Centre for Contemporary Cultural Studies in Birmingham, England, in 1964 and published their groundbreaking texts in the mid-1970s. Comprised of young, enthusiastic British scholars such as Stuart Hall, Tony Jefferson, and Dick Hebdige, the Birmingham School was engaged in a collaborative effort to look closely at young people and take what they were doing seriously. Youth subculture, they argued, was not just an expression of generational nonconformity,[4] but rather a process by which new cultural forms were created that could be manifest in specific subcultures, like the teddy boys, the mods, the rockers, and the punks.[5]

It's important to note that these scholars were also committed Marxists, so their work focused on reading the symbols of subculture style to discover their political meaning. The central idea was that working-class youths' styles could be read as symbolic expressions of resistance. Youth accomplished this, they argued, by reordering symbols—acts they called "bricolage," a term borrowed from cultural anthropology[6]—which created new meaning systems. They argued that these acts, being purely symbolic, could not significantly alter the lives of youth subculture participants, but nevertheless, through this process they were able to "win space" from the larger society. They saw this as a reaction to the ideological imperative of postwar capitalism, in which youth were forced to construct identities based on consumption practices.

The Birmingham School's use of bricolage remains useful for understanding how many subcultures make sense of their worlds. Bricolage was used to explain the way in which various subcultures reworked products of capitalism for their own use. Graffiti writers transform spray paint from a household product into a tool to create devastating art. They also use the subways and walls of the world's cities as media spaces, a purpose they were never intended to serve. Skateboarders manipulate urban architecture, transforming everyday space into a place for creative physical performances.[7] In terms of fashion, bricolage illuminates the transgressive power behind hip hop legends Eric B. and Rakim's homemade Gucci warm-up suits, which they wore on the cover of their second album, *Follow the Leader*.[8] It also explains how the obsession of the shoplifting crew the Brooklyn Lo-Lifes with Polo clothes transforms the meaning of that brand from country club elite to hip hop cool.[9]

The Birmingham School's influence has been far reaching, inspiring many researchers to address the meaning of politics and style in youth subcultures. It also is a lightning-rod for criticism. Over the years they have been criticized for their lack of ethnographic specificity; for failing to recognize the internal racial, class, and gender diversity of subcultures; for overemphasizing resistance; for ignoring the role of young women and entrepreneurialism; and for insisting that even the slightest commercial success was evidence of cooptation.[10]

More recently, a group of U.K. scholars, many of whom had been punks themselves, came of age and began to reassess the legacy of the Birmingham School. They have dubbed their work, which attempts to update subculture studies in the wake of postmodern thought, post-subcultural studies. David Muggleton, one of the pioneers in the construction of post-subcultural theory, grew up in the punk subculture in England and realized that he saw little of his own experience in the pages of Dick Hebdige's classic *Subculture: The Meaning of Style*.[11] At first he attributed this to his inability to understand the dense theory. However, as a university student he reread Hebdige and, as he relays it, "[I] understood exactly what he meant, and *still* found that it had very little to say about my life!"[12]

Post-subcultural studies is an emerging perspective that encompasses a broad range of thinking about subcultures. Its practitioners are united in their criticism of the Birmingham position that style could be read only as resistance. The core texts of post-subcultural studies include the work of Muggleton, Steve Redhead, Rupert Weinzierl, and Paul Hodkinson, all of whom were influenced by the insightful work on club cultures by Sarah Thornton, who applied Pierre Bordieu's concept of cultural capital to subcultural worlds and taste cultures.[13] These scholars represent a broad international perspective. However, their work has had relatively little influence among sociologists and criminologists in the United States, where the question of youth subculture and style remains exclusive to disciplines like American studies (the notable texts include *Generations of Youth* and *Microphone Fiends*).[14] The goal of this new literature is to acknowledge the legacy of the Birmingham School while completely reassessing it.

By far the most consistent criticism leveled at the Birmingham School theorists is that despite all of their sophisticated theory, their positions couldn't really be supported on the ground. In other words, we can never really be sure if 1970s subcultures were as exclusively working-class and re-sistant as the Birmingham scholars claim because they never really asked anyone who was a subculture participant. This is Muggleton's main line of critique. He argues that with the "exception of [Paul] Willis," their greatest "theoretical inadequacy" was their "failure to take seriously the subjective viewpoints of the subculturalists themselves."[15] Rather, he insists that re-searchers should seek to understand how people articulate their own social worlds.

The emerging field of cultural criminology is similarly committed to exploring the subjective worlds of subcultures, but these scholars do not root subculture participation completely in symbolic resistance or post-modern identity formation.[16] Rather, cultural criminologists explore the meaning systems that produce ideas about crime and criminals. They un-derstand that media and other outlets of popular culture help to define ideas about what is a crime and who is a criminal. Cultural criminology therefore views subcultural participation not only as against the main-stream, but as something that very often comes to be defined as criminal, as in the cases of graffiti writing and skateboarding.[17]

However, for those doing crimes, crime is not only a means for sur-vival, or even resistance—it is sometimes merely enjoyable. Heavily influ-enced by Jack Katz's *Seductions of Crime*, cultural criminologists recognize that youth are attracted to many of these deviant, illicit subcultures not only to solve problems or resist domination, but also because these activi-ties can be quite thrilling. First and foremost, writing graffiti is fun—and part of what makes it fun is that it's against the law. It can be exciting to get away with what Katz calls "sneaky crime" that "frequently thrills its practitioners."[18] I would argue that writers are aware of the ways in which writing is a *constructed* crime. Many writers embrace the excitement and thrill of "getting up" illegally, but they do so with a sense of righteousness. It's almost as if writers believe that graffiti is not a crime; but at the same time, I think many would also cease writing if graffiti were suddenly made legal. In fact, writers who only do legal walls are usually ridiculed despite often exhibiting impressive styles.

Scholars like Jeff Ferrell, Keith Hayward, Jock Young, Wayne Morri-son, and Mike Presdee recognize that subcultural activity in and of itself is not political. They argue that the political significance of subculture is the way those who participate in the subculture highlight the contested and shifting boundaries between illegal and legal activities.

As noted earlier, the criminality of what Ferrell calls "crimes of style"[19] is imbedded in a set of cultural practices that often require a coordinated media and public relations campaign to force the public to see them as a serious crime. Graffiti, however, depending on the context, can be legal or illegal, crime or art, vandalism or community service. This complexity is one key to understanding how writers can make a career of their activities, and it indicates a unique relationship between crime and the paths to adulthood and legitimate success.[20]

While contemporary scholars have done an excellent job of dragging subculture studies into the postmodern era, even these conceptions cannot account for cultures like graffiti. Many of these scholars focus on passionate fans of particular music genres who dress to identify themselves as such. These scholars use the term "subculture," along with a host of other terms, including "taste cultures," "club cultures," and "neo-tribes," to describe the styles and communities of like-minded listeners, thus excluding cultures like graffiti.[21]

Graffiti writing is distinctly different from those cultures whose members spend most of their time dressing up. Writers do not dress to impress; instead, they want you to notice their names in public spaces because of how often and how stylishly they write it. For music subcultures, membership is based upon taste, appearance, and social relationships, while for graffiti writers it is based upon your deeds. Gender, race, class, personal style, sexuality, taste in music, and social networks are all secondary to "getting up," having one's graffiti name seen in public space.[22] Graffiti is not a spectacular culture in the tradition of mods or punks. Graffiti writers do not have a style of dress that announces to the larger society that they are part of a subculture. Graffiti writing is unique in that writers are anonymous and don't use their real names in their tags. Non-writers have a very hard time identifying a graffiti writer when they are not writing. Writers also have the option of choosing how, when, and to whom they reveal their secret identities.[23]

Although the post-subcultural scholars have made progress in the theorization of subculture and its relationship to postmodern identity formation, it is still not clear where a culture like graffiti, which has no dress code and no soundtrack, fits into this paradigm. The literature focuses almost exclusively on music and fashion and has very little to say about non-music subcultures. Of course, this doesn't stop them from appropriating graffiti for their own use. For example, the book cover of *The Post-Subcultures Reader* features a photo of a graffiti b-boy, yet there is not a single mention of graffiti in the entire collection of essays.[24]

Further, subcultural and even post-subcultural studies treat youth subculture participation as something one does when one is young. These positions take it as a given that youth subculture is something that one leaves as one ages. While many have argued about the significance of subcultural style, whether as symbolic resistance or as a facilitator of postmodern identity, few have theorized the impact that youth subculture participation has on the members themselves as they move into adulthood.

As noted earlier, graffiti writers, like many young people, moderate their deviance as they approach adulthood. Many writers, however, depend on their participation in an illegal subculture for their income. Those who have built a reputation and avoided arrest find that they can use their talent, knowledge, and fame to transition into an adult career. While "desistance" research shows that most young people turn away from crime as they approach their thirties and instead settle into adult roles, it cannot account for the fact that participation in an illegal subculture nurtured their talents and helped them to find careers.

Most scholars assert that as one grows older, subcultural membership will either cease or lead to more serious forms of criminality. While it is obvious that success in a subculture leads to increased status within the subculture, little work has been done to try and understand how participants in youth subcultures create adult lives. Kids who write graffiti and are good at it have a very good chance of becoming successful adults. There are many reasons for this, from the psychological benefits of fame and respect, to the way in which writing and writers teach each other about art, or the way in which clever young people understand that there is a market for their transgressive activity.

Despite the enormous critical attention focused on the Birmingham School, the post-subcultural studies scholars missed one very essential point. The Birmingham scholars argued that the media would co-opt any subcultural style, and eventually the corporate economy would market that style to the masses. Since there were no careers that kids could make from their subculture experiences, they would be forced back into the drudgery of working-class adulthood.[25] They argued that the politics of subculture style was only symbolic; it did not solve the larger structural problems facing working-class people. In *Resistance through Rituals*, Hall and Jefferson write:

The problematic of a subordinate class experience can be "lived through" negotiated or resisted; but it cannot be resolved at that level or by those means. There is no "subcultural career" for the working class lad, no "solution" in the subcultural milieu, for problems posed by the key structuring experiences of the class.[26]

This criticism of the subculture approach has yet to be fully addressed. What if today's subcultures are a path toward future success? Punks, writers, skaters, hip-hoppers, and goths have all made careers out of their subcultural experiences. The idea that subculture participation might actually be beneficial to young people must be taken into account in future theories of subculture. Even for those "grounded theorists" like Muggleton, subculture style is an example of a pastiched, postmodern identity. But whether or not this identity might better equip young people to live as adults in a postmodern world is not assessed.

While it may be an oversimplification to assess subculture on a normative level, most subculture scholars have predicted that bad things were in store for these bad kids, and this is simply not the case. These kids are bad, indeed, but as RUN-DMC would put it, "Not bad meaning bad, but BAD MEANING GOOD." This characterization of subculture as a place where bad makes good comes from my own ethnographic commitment to graffiti culture, which has lasted for over a decade. I have witnessed kids in their teens and twenties going "wild in the streets" only to become righteous, successful adults. In much of the subculture and post-subculture literature, this issue is always framed in terms of cooptation and selling out, but I would argue that even the Birmingham School would find it difficult to criticize the success of completely self-made young people.

While there are trace elements in the deviant literature that subcultural participation can lead to careers, few if any scholars have described the impact of youth culture into the adult years. Many who have participated in subcultures have used this experience to become upwardly mobile. While this may not have had the political impact that Birmingham School scholars had hoped for, it is the case that many kids found creative ways to survive into adulthood. The Birmingham School scholars would likely argue that subcultures have been completely coopted by corporations and that they are used to distract many working-class youth whose energies could be focused elsewhere. My research shows otherwise.

While some in the academy might lament the fact that subculture careers are not necessarily political, at least some of those kids whose opportunities were limited have found ways to make their lives interesting and productive. The options for subculturalists are not simply prison or selling out.

CAREER OPPORTUNITIES

Rewriting Subculture Resistance

The idea of an adult career is critical to understanding youth culture in the twenty-first century. There are skateboarders, rappers, graffiti muralists, BMX freestyle bikers, and DJs making enough money to live well and provide for themselves and their families. These cultures also produce careers within the culture that arise to fill the need for documentation and dissemination of information. Within the culture of graffiti writers, there are not only kids who make money directly as muralists and fine artists, but also indirectly as magazine editors, journalists, photographers, graphic designers, and marketing firms, just to name a few.

The notion of career is not new to the study of subculture. Becker used the term "deviant career" to describe the activities of an individual who "sustains a pattern of deviance over a long period of time, who makes deviance a way of life."[1] Becker clearly does not mean to imply that people make a living from their deviance. To highlight those who make money from their deviant lifestyles, he describes those who have "careers in a deviant occupational group."[2] For jazz musicians who play music for a paying audience, the tension between subcultural insiders and outsiders is once again brought up. In order to be successful, musicians are forced to cater to the tastes of the listeners, what they call "going commercial." Here there is a recognition that in order to make money, one must concede some amount of artistic integrity in order to please the uneducated public. Jazzmen are constantly making compromises between jobs that allow them to play real jazz, but pay little, and those commercial jobs that allow them security and opportunities for more prestige and income. Every musician must negotiate this tension for themselves, but it is clear that few, if any, can afford to play only jazz. Those who can't bear to compromise often leave music altogether.[3]

Career success can only be achieved by some degree of distance from the subculture. Selling out was a key idea of the Birmingham School, so that any effort by punks to get money was treated as a sign of cooptation by the mainstream. Similarly, they understood the way in which the media and other outlets for profit would coopt subcultural style and sell it to the masses, thus deflating the movement of any of its initial resistance, symbolic or otherwise. While Becker would claim that those who attain commercial success as jazz musicians are still members of a deviant occupational subculture, Birmingham scholars would claim that financial success voids their subculture status because their actions are no longer seen as political resistance. For Becker it is not an all-or-nothing game. As shown, jazz musicians are constantly finessing the boundaries between artistic and financial success. However, both notions treat success as a logical distancing from some notion of original artistic purity or political power. Further success always occurs to greater and lesser degrees outside of the borders of the subculture.

In Richard Lachmann's "Graffiti as Career and Ideology,"[4] he uses Becker's term "deviant career" to describe the time individuals spent writing graffiti, and he uses Becker's concept of "art world" (1982) to highlight the collective production of art that takes place within the subculture.[5] Lachmann applies Becker's thesis, arguing that individuals learn graffiti art through interactions with other artists in a complex set of mentoring relationships, where older writers teach younger writers techniques and aesthetic standards.[6] Becker argues further that art making is also facilitated by those "resource pools" outside the subculture who provide materials, supplies, and financial success.[7]

Lachmann discusses two periods when graffiti writers were pursued by gallery owners who were not members of the subculture. He argues that the production of graffiti art on canvas subscribed to the general qualities of an art world.[8] Art making involves not only artists, but suppliers, dealers, critics, gallery owners, and art buyers. This requires some amount of adaptation to the tastes of the audience. As with jazz musicians, this means that in some ways consumers of the culture help to define the aesthetics and also regulate rewards and punishments.

Lachmann describes how "entrepreneurs served as intermediaries, packaging graffiti muralists and their work in ways that appealed to journalists and gallery owners. . . . Dealers skirted the aesthetic merits of graffiti art in their sales pitches and instead contrasted the artists' background of poverty and crime with their current ability to 'paint just like real trained artists.'"[9]

Lachmann argues that the destruction by police of writers' benches (subway stations like 149th Street, where writers congregated to view and discuss the work on the trains) severed the communal links between writers.[10] This allowed for the commodification of graffiti art in the 1980s, and for Lachmann this effectively ended artists' relationship with the gallery scene. He identifies the *Post-Graffiti Show* in SoHo in 1983 as marking the end of this period. Lachmann concludes his article where this book might have begun; he writes, "After the collapse of the graffiti art market in 1983, none of the muralists returned to subway or neighborhood art. A few quit entirely; the others sought to enroll in art schools or make careers as graphic artists."[11]

As a result of this experience with gallery owners and mainstream media, graffiti culture turned inward. This was complemented by advances in the democratization of technology that allowed writers to communicate and disseminate their work over a vast geographical expanse. The community effectively became both the consumers and the producers of graffiti art and all things related, from canvasses to magazines to caps and supplies like the ink created and distributed by graffiti writer KR. This formation of a semi-autonomous market has provided writers with careers in the production, dissemination, and documentation of graffiti art. The collective processes that formerly took place outside of the subculture now occur primarily within it, directed primarily by those who have practiced the form. This development allowed graffiti writers in the 1990s to insulate themselves somewhat from complete exploitation and appropriation by corporations.

Today, writers' success as gallery artists occurs within a set of overlapping subcultures. Skaters, writers, and other street artists have gained the attention, once again, of the mainstream art world, but this time their work is judged according to aesthetic standards, not simply on the tough circumstances from which the individual artists emerged. Stars like Margaret Kilgallen and Barry McGee have shown their work in the Whitney Museum of American Art and Ryan McGinness has work in the permanent collection of the Museum of Modern Art. All of these folks can be found in the book *Beautiful Losers: Contemporary Art and Street Culture*, which documents these emerging talents.[12] While there are certainly collectors outside of these cultures that are buying this art, many of the buyers for these works are other successful writers, skaters, and artists. Ed Templeton, pro skater and gallery artist, recently purchased a Steve Powers work for an undisclosed amount, showing that some of the money generated in the subculture stays there.

As discussed above, the current crop of British subculture scholars understand that it is possible to make money from subculture participation.

However, their analysis of subculture career opportunities is limited in scope because it tends to focus narrowly on fashion and identity.

Here in the States, Robin Kelley describes the creative ways in which young African-Americans have turned their play into work and gotten paid.[13] Rappers have gone from rapping at parties in the park to performing sold-out shows all over the world—or, as Jay-Z says, "from Marcy [projects] to Madison Square [Garden]." This again brings up the issue of selling out, but it is nevertheless significant that disadvantaged youth all over the world have taken their fun into adulthood and made lives for themselves. While some youthful pursuits like music and team sports have a corporate structure in place ready to profit from others' talents, graffiti culture has had a semi-autonomous micro-industry that has been somewhat safe from corporate takeover. However, these days may be short-lived. As I write this, COPE2 is doing sneakers for Converse and HAZE has designed a color scheme for a Scion, while fashion mogul Mark Ecko has produced a video game titled "Getting Up: Contents Under Pressure." I do not intend to suggest that any of these writers have sold out graffiti culture. In fact, they are pioneers who have brought greater awareness to the power of this medium, and the ultimate result may be more opportunities for more young people and less hassle from the police and politicians.

The Foundations of the Subculture Career

Writers' first opportunities at success came when they were invited into the economic apparatus of the art world. Graffiti writers started painting canvases for art dealers in the early 1980s, yet the sums of money these generated are rarely discussed. However, even though no one was getting rich, this did let writers know that it was possible to be taken seriously as artists (even if it wasn't in their home countries). Many of the second-generation of subway superstars, including BLADE, SEEN, DONDI, CRASH, QUIK, NOC, and LEE, were doing group shows in Europe throughout the 1980s.[14]

As the decade wore on, politicians continued to wage war on writers and for outside collectors the novelty of graffiti on canvas began to wear off. By 1989 the public art show that had run on New York City subways had ceased and the gallery opportunities, especially in the United States, were also drying up.

But writers kept writing, and they were good. On walls, on clean trains that never ran, and in secret tunnels, they continued to progress.

Many of these writers had become excellent self-taught artists and were encouraged by some sympathetic adults (e.g., high school counselors) to put portfolios together with photos and sketches of their graffiti work and apply to college.

This is a very significant point that receives little or no attention. Many of the first- and second-generation post-subway graffiti writers have been to college—ESPO, KR, VERT, AME, PSOUP, KEST, DES, AMAZE, CYCLE, HUSH, and KAWS, to name a few. With few options to become artists in the late 1980s and early 1990s, these writers all went off to college. There they expanded their repertoires and learned many of the skills that would help them to start magazines and retail businesses and become fine artists, all of which increased the career options for adults who were successful graffiti writers as youth. However, the graffiti career is not limited only to those who go to college.

The magazine phenomenon came about naturally as the culture grew and the technology became more readily available. Writers in numerous cities around the country and the world wanted to know who was doing what, so they began to trade flicks. The photos could be copied and passed around. When the technology caught up, the kids used it to put these photos in self-produced 'zines, and thus the documentation of graffiti became a product that writers would pay a small sum for.

This gave writers a chance to utilize other skills, such as journalistic writing, graphic design, and marketing, further expanding the opportunities beyond the vapors of aerosol.[15] Some graffiti artists painted murals, some moved onto canvases and metal, while others who didn't have the talent or desire to paint into adulthood used their skills in other areas, like photography, fashion design, writing, computer graphics, and web design.

While membership in the subculture requires proficiency in the form, the subculture career extends beyond expertise in the form itself. It's not only the superstars who are able to make careers for themselves. The need for documentation produced a graffiti micro-media staffed by current and former graffiti writers. It is important to understand this in the context of our postindustrial world. Many of these young people were destined for blue-collar or white-collar servitude. These kids refused the meager options presented to them by the larger society, and instead perfected extremely risky cultural pursuits. Their success in this form eventually opened up other opportunities, and today those efforts are paying off, literally.

The subculture career counters the common perception of graffiti writers as vandals bent on a life of crime, and instead focuses on the ways that people turn these experiences into something positive. Despite all of the forces acting against them, many successful writers do big things. The skills and commitment required to be a successful graffiti writer provide many with the confidence that they can indeed excel within and beyond the subculture and turn out to be pretty successful adults.

I asked Steve Powers what he thought about all of this in an email, and he responded with the following:

> School provided me with a discipline that I wasn't developing on my own, but I was a terrible student and only 1 or 2 teachers would've bet that I would continue as an artist. I was looking for a bridge between graff and high art, but I couldn't ask my teachers. I had too much graffiti on the street (and in the hallways and elevators) to risk it. So I did my research in private. It was only when I met TWIST that I saw process was the key. Years before that, when I started *On the Go*, I wanted to become a functioning adult because it hadn't been done in Philly. I had no role models that managed to turn graff into something productive after the age of 20. And I did have friends that wanted what I wanted. At first, having a career wasn't a real possibility, it was the idea that staying creative and working hard would yield positive results.

TIMMY TATTOO

Timmy's Long Island Tattoo Shop

Tim was the first writer who took an active role in this project, but he also was the least active on the streets. Tim graduated from the School of Visual Arts in 1995 and spent most of his time trying to figure out what to do with his life. Eventually he settled on tattooing, a path that other graffiti writers had pioneered a generation before him. In the last ten years or so Tim has gotten really good, and we've remained close friends. When my parents returned from Ireland and brought back the family crest from my Mother's side of the family (the Moores from County Cork), I decided that this would be a fine tattoo to get from Timmy, who is an excellent artist and also proud of his Irish heritage. After exchanging a few emails of the proposed design, we decided on May 9, 2005, at his house in Brooklyn. I told Tim that I wanted to ask him some questions for the book while he was tattooing me, but the excitement of getting a shiny new tattoo and the drone of the tattoo machine made questioning difficult. This would be my second tattoo, and since my first was in 1991 I couldn't really remember how much pain there was. This tattoo was going to be 500 percent larger, and I knew that it was going to require a bit of stamina.

I tried to get some info from Tim as he was setting up, and Tim brought up what I said to him years ago when we were coworkers at the restaurant. He told me back then that he had just purchased a tattoo machine and was going to become a tattoo artist. At that time Timmy had no tattoos himself, and he was showing me a very sketchy rendition of the Morton Salt girl he had done on his leg. Tim says that I told him, "You can't just DO tattoos—it takes practice, and like ten years to get good at it." "Well," Timmy said, smiling, "Here you are almost ten years later."

"I guess I was waiting for you to perfect you craft," I said.

I couldn't tell if Tim was suggesting that I had lacked faith in him and told him that my advice was intended as encouragement rather than discouragement. Tim said that I was right, tattooing had been a lot harder than he thought.

After graduating with a degree in illustration from the School of Visual Arts, Tim was confused about breaking into the world of illustration. He tried unsuccessfully to get jobs illustrating for other people's books and even did some comic books, but all of these efforts required organizing with other people and, worse, waiting for their judgment. Tim says he likes tattoos because they are immediate and permanent. You create, you please your client, and you get paid. There are no boards or groups of people or gallerists or dealers judging his work; he has one simple and direct goal, please his client, get paid. Sometimes it's beautiful art, sometimes mere craftwork, sometimes it's even kind of dumb, but there is no confusion. Tim finds this to be extremely satisfying and as a result he has gotten very, very good.

Tim has also changed his body. He is now covered with colorful tattoos from a slew of famous artists, and I ask him about them all as he slowly sets up his tools and inks until he's ready to get to work. I hear the buzz of the machine, and wait in anticipation for it to touch my skin, and when it does the pain isn't so bad at all. I'm relieved. My maternal grandparents, Harold and Jayne Moore, have passed, and since they had three girls the Moore name will be lost in our family, so I've made it my part to carry it on. Tim, being Irish, knows full well the significance of this.

Tim got the black outline on my left arm in about an hour and I was extremely pleased. Next he started laying out the colors. He said he had a vision of how my tattoo was going to look and there was to be no consultation. Every time I tried to inquire what he was doing he would say, "I've got a plan," so I just sat back and marveled at his confidence. When he was finished I had a big, green crest with a lion in the middle. Tim's first comments were, "Now we're gonna have to do the other arm, that little tattoo you have looks silly compared to the size of the crest."

In 2000 Timmy started working at Cliff's Tattoo Shop in Long Island. Cliff had four locations around Long Island, and it was getting to be too much work, so in 2006 Tim worked out a deal to buy the Huntington shop. Now Tim has two artists working for him and he makes a good living doing what he likes to do. As a way of marking Tim's success I went out to Long Island to get another tattoo and to write Timmy's subculture career onto my body. This time I went bigger and even more complex and put myself more completely in Timmy's hands. I had chosen a rainbow trout, again to honor my maternal grandfather, but also to get a tattoo that would really let Timmy showcase his artistic skills; besides, in Japanese tattoo lore, fish are good luck. I needed some good luck[1] and felt that by getting a new tattoo I would force myself to deal with the psychological trepidation that comes with a change in one's life. It took nearly four hours but Timmy completed a beautiful piece, and when I asked him how much I should pay, he said he had a hard time charging friends and family.

That's just the type of guy that Timmy is. He is fiercely talented, honest and fair, and completely without pretension. He does not have a huge ego as a superstar tattoo artist, and he is very humble when discussing his success. However, Tim now owns his own business and has done it all through simple perseverance.

In late August Tim and his fiancée Margaret contacted Alma and I because they wanted help planning their wedding. We had had our wedding in October and Timmy and Margaret wanted to do the same. When it became clear that they meant that they thought they could plan a wedding in two months, we told them to come over right away so we could set them straight. They wound up getting married in March 2007 in a beautiful ceremony in Connecticut, and all of Tim's graffiti friends, including AME and PSOUP, were in attendance. This project began with graffiti and now our lives our intertwined, and I've been marked for life.

On a cold Saturday afternoon in December 2007 I went out to visit Timmy in his shop. I arrived around 4:00, and Tim was hard at work finishing up a large tattoo on the arm of a Long Island construction worker. The client had been patiently enduring the pain since about 12:30 and Tim finally finished up around 5:00. He ate a slice of pizza and took a twenty-minute break and then got back to work on the next client, which took him until about 7 P.M. For these two pieces Timmy received approximately seven hundred dollars. Lots of this money goes to expenses and supplies, but I left assured that my friend was a happy and successful adult.

GABE BANNER

Market Wise

Gabe Banner, thirty, is a five-foot-eight white Jewish male whose tattooed arms and legs identify him as someone who grew up in the hardcore music scene. He is also an ex-graffiti writer who worked for *On the Go* magazine. This experience taught him to think strategically about how to reach people by any means, regardless of budget. Today he uses these skills to help major corporations develop and execute marketing strategies. When asked by his clients what he can do for them, he responds with a litany of strategies that are reminiscent of the tactics he employed in his younger years. "Figure out who you want to reach, and where they are. Figure out what you want them to respond to, and then decide on a strategy to get maximum exposure for your time and money."[1]

Gabe's introduction to alternative subcultures started with skateboarding and punk rock in the late 1980s and early 1990s in the suburbs of Washington, D.C. A friend of his, Matt Kuehl, had an older sister, Sara, who was working on a dissertation on the emerging D.C. graffiti scene. Matt and his bandmates had recently begun tagging and convinced Gabe that he needed to come up with a tag of his own. Matt wrote a tag on a bench in front of the movie theater on Wisconsin Avenue and Gabe followed suit. Graffiti quickly became part of Gabe's teenage life; however, he was isolated from the larger movement, confessing that they really didn't know what graffiti was. They hadn't seen *Subway Art*, *Wild Style*, *Video Graf*, or even any real pieces. Throughout the 1990s, Gabe (along with early partners MARE, REAL, and HOME) discovered more and more sites throughout Washington, like the Aqueducts in Georgetown, which served as his graffiti primer course. Gabe says that the first real piece he saw was by CYCLE, a transplanted Connecticut writer going to art school in D.C. CYCLE helped pioneer spots like the Aqueducts and D.C.'s Graffiti Hall of Fame, also called "Art Under Pressure," along with SMK,

DOSE, DAH, CHA, RUST, and others, and was influential in the emerging D.C. graffiti scene.[2]

Gabe's crew of graffiti, punk rock kids were, as he says, "a pretty diverse group of kids from the suburbs." Relatively speaking, Gabe didn't have the resources of some of his peers, however he was able to attend private school in Bethesda because his mom taught there and he received financial aid and was assisted by his grandparents. These suburban kids with money and cars from their parents were "runnin' wild in the streets," yet for the most part they got good grades.

Gabe eventually came up with the name KEST and got good enough to be down with the most prestigious crew in D.C., NAA (New Age Artists). Throughout high school Gabe wrote graffiti, played drums in various hardcore bands, booked and promoted shows, and still maintained his grades. His parents gave him a lot of freedom, but this freedom wasn't necessarily contingent upon doing well in school. He reveals that he abused his parents, saying he "walked all over them." Instead, he attributes his grades to the culture of the upper-middle-class private school he attended. His folks never insisted he do well in school, he just did. He does, however, come from good intellectual stock; his father is a former molecular biologist and pianist and his mother is an artist and former art teacher at his elementary school. For Gabe, academic success came easy. Unlike KAWS, ESPO, AME, and others, graffiti was not a last-ditch effort to get into college as an art student. Gabe scored a 1220 on his SATs and decided to move to New York City to attend New York University, which he financed with the help of his grandparents and lots of financial aid.

Gabe wasn't interested in becoming an artist. He enrolled in NYU's College of Arts and Sciences and began to soak up the energy and excitement of the city. He took the required classes (rarely attending) and then took "Teen Culture" with Professor Lyn Pentecost in the Metropolitan Studies Department. He was inspired to find a professor who was into the same things he was: punk rock, graffiti, and hip hop. He took every one of her classes and eventually majored in metropolitan studies, with a minor in journalism.

Throughout his first year of school, Gabe continued to write KEST and enjoyed New York as a graffiti playground, but writing without a crew to back him up proved to be a challenge. Graffiti is about fame and beef, and as soon as you get a little fame, beef is sure to follow. Gabe wrote with a few kids who had his back, but he had to make a choice between defending the name KEST and having to rely on kids he didn't really like. He got word that someone else was writing KEST and wanted to battle him. They would both do pieces and the best piece would win and get the title to the name. However, Gabe heard that this was a ruse and that the dude was going to stab him or rob him. Gabe figured wisely, that the guys he was writing with probably were not to be trusted, so he cut ties with them and decided that even if he could win one fight it probably wouldn't end there. Beef often escalates, and he didn't have a big enough crew to squash the beef so he slowed down his writing.

As Gabe became less active writing graffiti, he immersed himself more fully into graffiti culture. He was an avid consumer of graffiti magazines like *On the Go*, and he began to expand his peer group. A friend of Gabe's worked for *On the Go* as their bike messenger and when he left, Gabe took over the job. Gabe was excited to be part of *OTG* and gladly ran errands for publishers Ari Forman and Steve Powers, who quickly became his mentors. Even though he wasn't writing graffiti, he knew that he could learn a lot from these extremely talented dudes. Ari soon took Gabe under his wing, schooling him in the magazine business and constantly lecturing Gabe on what it took to be successful.

On the Go had great ways of marketing itself directly to its demographic. They would make full stickers out of their upcoming covers and send three or four trusted colleagues, including Gabe, out into the streets to put the stickers up in spots where graffiti writers tagged.

The magazine ran into financial difficulties, and companies became less interested in buying ads. However, the same companies were curious about the techniques *OTG* was using to market itself. Foreman, the art director, had a vision and was focused. He was doing freelance graphic design for a company called DNA, and he convinced one of its partners to invest in a small business called On the Go Marketing. Its mission was to bring non-traditional marketing strategies to mainstream companies. Gabe had just graduated from college and Ari called him up and told him that he had a job for him. Thus began Gabe's transition away from graffiti writing and into the world of non-traditional marketing.

Gabe began working in earnest for On the Go Marketing in 1999. There his duties eventually expanded from the very basic (putting up stickers) to include campaign creation, budgeting, and project management. Ari schooled Gabe not only in how to maximize exposure and stretch a dollar, but also in the nuances of the marketing game.

In 2003, after a particularly bad experience, Gabe and On the Go had had enough of each other. Their recently appointed president, a mayor of a small town in New Jersey, butted heads immediately with Gabe when, within his first week, he had tried to fire two stellar employees whom Gabe had hired. Gabe decided it was time for him to move on.

However, Gabe's introduction to marketing at the scrappy young company had fortuitously generated a real interest in the marketing and advertising world. Gabe knew that this was the type of work he wanted, and he eventually landed at LIME, the public relations and promotions wing of Kirshenbaum, Bond + Partners, a midsized advertising agency in SoHo. There he helped produce a temporary art gallery for Sharp Electronics that sought to gain acceptance with a young, downtown crowd. Today Gabe continues to work for LIME and enjoys it immensely despite the hectic hours and busy schedule, and he remains a close friend.

ESPO/STEVE POWERS

Dreamland Artist Club

In the summer of 2005 Steve Powers invited me to spend some time with him at his new sign shop and studio in Coney Island, New York. I was a bit confused, but when ESPO says he's into something new, it always winds up being a rewarding experience. As I approached Steve was pushing up the clean roll-down gate on the front of his shop on Surf Avenue, which is called the Dreamland Artist Club after the project that Steve began with the help of the public art organization Creative Time. The project started when Steve was walking the streets of Coney Island and approached the owner of the El Dorado Bumper Cars and asked if he could paint their famous brown and yellow "Bump Ya Ass Off" sign that hangs in the entrance. He told them he didn't want money, only the opportunity to paint a new one, and they agreed to let him. Soon the other businesses wanted fresh signs, and Steve saw an opportunity. He got Creative Time involved and suggested that they invite some young, up-and-coming artists to give Coney Island new signs. Steve insisted that this was not just an opportunity for artists to use the space for their own art; they had to be creating signs that would help the businesses that needed them, and they had to do work within the context of the iconography of Coney Island. To date Steve and other artists have painted about twenty such signs. Additionally, Steve was able to repaint all of the cars on the iconic Cyclone Roller Coaster, a symbol synonymous with New York City, and, as far as graffiti writers are concerned, the equivalent of repainting the Sistine Chapel. Steve is humble and attributes his ultimate act of "getting over" to the fact that no one else ever asked.

When Steve first painted the El Dorado sign, graffiti writers recognized ESPO's style and were amazed that he had gotten up on this level. Yet Steve had always been doing graffiti this way. In 1998 and 1999 Steve

ESPO, early illegal signage, Lower East Side.

would scour New York City for abandoned businesses and repaint their signs with his name.

His interest in painting illegal graffiti signs eventually evolved into a passion for sign painting. Sign painters, with their intricate freehand lettering and speed of execution, share skills with graffiti writers. Steve's studio art reflects these interests. This aesthetic style is also a way of staying close to letters, something most former graffiti writers leave behind when they move on to become "real" artists.

In September 2007 Steve sent out a mass email that the Dreamland Artist Club had lost its lease and would be closing soon, and that he would be hosting a "closing"/preview of new work party and that all of the art work he had done there for the last two years would be up for sale. It is difficult to grasp just how successful Steve has become and how much his work is selling for these days. Steve is represented by the Deitch Gallery, and he has sold single pieces for between fifteen and twenty thousand dollars. I decided that I wanted a piece to honor the end of this study, but that I could only afford five hundred dollars, which would still take a significant bite out of my paycheck from Baruch College.

On Saturday afternoon, September 20, before leaving for Coney Island to check out Steve's art work, I wrote out and signed a check to Stephen Powers, and my plan was just to give it to him and let him pick something for me. I had no expectations about what this would bring me.

My wife Alma and I arrived at the Dreamland Artist Club around 6 P.M. and were greeted by KR, an old friend and now successful writer, artist, and ink manufacturer in his own right, who informed us that lots of good pieces had already been sold. We greeted Steve, who was dressed in a white Izod polo shirt and khaki Polo Rugby golf pants with skulls where the golf bags should be. His trademark "Eraserhead" high fade haircut was in full effect. Young people in their twenties were milling about looking at Steve's work, which decorated the shop. There were pieces painted on yellow sign metal hung in the front window, on the walls, on the arched ceiling, and in the bathroom. This work is painted with "One Spot" sign paint, which can't be blended with other paints and is similar to working with aerosol, ultimately limiting the range of color at Steve's disposal.

I gave Steve my check and he started walking around the room. "Let's see," he said, "you've been a long time supporter." Now it was not my intention to low-ball Steve, nor was I trying to get a deal; I was simply giving him what I could almost afford and was trying to skip the process of having to ask for prices. I liked all the work, but Steve picked up the custom raincoat he made that was written up in the *New York Times*.[1] The yellow raincoat has black and red leaves adorning the front; the back has a black book of matches juxtaposed with a red can of gasoline and is adorned with the tag line "Be My Co-Defendant." Steve and I have come a long way since we first met, and we both now share a passion

ESPO, gas station, Chelsea.

The author in a coat by ESPO.

for ridiculous outfits. I get mine from the thrift stores, while Steve gets his for free from clothing manufacturers who understand his fame. Steve put the raincoat on me, and I was beaming. "Oh no, I couldn't," I said. I was a bit embarrassed, but also thrilled because I knew what these jackets cost. Steve originally was inspired by the jewelry flier guys on Canal Street, who wear vinyl sandwich boards to protect themselves from the weather. Steve decided to make them raincoats. In the meantime, clothing designer Mark Ecko wanted Steve to collaborate on a sweater design, so as part of his payment Steve got 150 classic yellow jackets made according to his exact specs. To date he had customized approximately six jackets with vinyl appliqués and said they were "extremely hard to do." They sold for $1,500, and wasn't sure how many he'd sold, but I couldn't believe that he was offering this one to me. Steve took me outside to photograph me in the new coat.

After the excitement of my new coat died down, I got back to ethnography. There was a good-looking Asian couple in their twenties and another Asian man of about the same age dressed in jeans and rare Nike sneakers. These folks were fans of Steve Powers the artist and had no real knowledge of the work he did in the streets nearly a decade ago. One prospective buyer was looking at 24 x 12 inch black ink drawings. Steve informed him that they went for $750, and it occurred to me that I couldn't even have afforded a painting. In fact my $500 was the cheapest sale that Steve made all day. The couple was expressing interest in a lot of Steve's work, and he was rattling off prices: $1,200, $2,000, $1,400—and these were sale prices. But to hear him tell it, he's by no

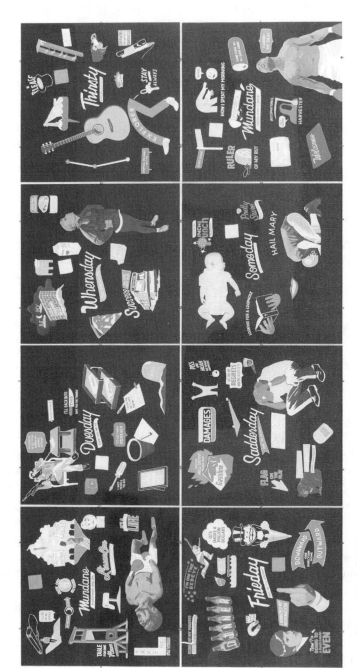

ESPO, "8 Day Week," 2007.

Steve Powers, postcard for the opening of
The Magic Word Exhibition, Pennsylvania Academy
of Fine Arts, October 20, 2007–January 27, 2008.

means rich. His supplies are incredibly expensive and he and his wife
have a new baby boy.

Steve was hard at work charming everyone, hosting a little party and
cracking wise at KR and I, who were locked in a conversation about red
wine and our best recipes. The couple who was expressing interest in pur-
chasing $5,000 worth of work had started to get into a heated discussion
about which pieces they wanted to buy. Steve let them know that he accepted credit cards and Pay Pal. These kids were smitten with ESPO, but
they said they needed to get something to eat and to discuss their potential purchases. Not wanting to lose the sale, Steve said, "Do you want to
leave your Master Card?" and she handed it to him. When they returned,
the dude handed Steve a massive wad of bills, $3,000 in cash, and told him
to take the rest from his Pay Pal account. The young woman spent $1,000
on two pieces in which Steve had appliquéd vinyl on plastic similar to the
raincoat.

Granted, these kids had purchased at least six pieces, but it was astounding that kids in their twenties could afford these prices. I found out that the young man owns a retail clothing shop in SoHo; he said he could not miss this opportunity to get some of Steve's art at these "affordable" prices. He wanted to put them in his gallery in the back of the store.

Steve packed up and signed all the stuff for these two young collectors, who had rented a mini-van to take home their haul. Steve's assistant brought in three six-packs of beer, and of course he was a former graffiti writer and emerging artist himself. When I told him that this book argues that graffiti writers can make adult careers, he agreed, saying that graffiti teaches you how to hustle and to go after what you really want. As the Asian couple got all their stuff into the mini-van, Steve turned to KR and me and said, "Fifteen grand, not a bad day."

I put on my ESPO raincoat and my wife and I headed out of the little studio and proceeded south on Stillwell avenue, past the El Dorado Bumper cars that Steve first painted two years ago. Two weeks later Stephen Powers had an exhibition at the Pennsylvania Academy of Fine Arts in Philadelphia. He premiered the "8 Day Week" panels that we had seen in progress at the Coney Island Shop. These pieces reflect a certain tragic-comic aspect of city life; trying to get by, procrastinating, struggling with substances, trying to maintain hope in the face of despair, and looking for salvation anywhere you can find it.

This show attracted attention in New York and Philly, and in the beginning of December he graced the cover of the art magazine *Juxtapose*, where they wrote, "In 10 years time, Stephen 'Espo' Powers' name will reside next to Crumb, Robert Williams, Basquiat, McGee and Warhol as those who truly changed the way art is defined and displayed. As 2007 comes to a close, we couldn't think of a better artist to honor."[2]

Once again I was blown away by all that Steve was doing, and it occurred to me that I am just as ignorant now of the world he lives in as I was the day he welcomed me into the culture of graffiti writing nearly eleven years ago.

CODA

Graffiti for Life

Stephen Powers has made a very successful transition into the art world. He has generated both critical acclaim and financial stability. His work continues many of the themes he began in the streets. A quick glance at the signs he paints these days shows that he continues to encourage us to create a narrative out of urban visual cacophony. Once again, there are stories being told. He continues to ask us to scrutinize our world.

Powers is an art star. Downtown hipsters and collectors with an eye to the future are buying up his paintings as investments. However, despite Steve's fame and success, he remains humble and generous with his time. He continues to help me progress as a writer, reading and critiquing many of my early drafts, and we continue to have conversations on a very high level. Steve recently published a new book, *First and Fifteenth: Pop Art Short Stories*, which focuses on constructing urban narratives out of everyday situations. He also recently won a Fulbright Grant to teach wall painting in some of the most impoverished neighborhoods in Dublin and Belfast, Ireland.

VERT's transition is also accompanied by a change in name. These days he goes by Timmy Tattoo. He owns and operates his own tattoo shop in Huntington, Long Island, following a path from graffiti to tattooing pioneered by early legends like SEEN. He does some graffiti tattoos, but his skills vary across a wide range of styles.

AME the monster graffiti talent is long gone. Matt's transitions were made through some very tumultuous college years. He switched from graphic design to painting to sculpture, where he excelled. Matt's biggest accomplishment through this time, though, was winning his battle with depression. He completed a two-year course in toy design at the Fashion Institute of Technology in New York City, but still has problems with the compromises involved in commercial success. He remains a thoughtful young man and a good friend.

Ironically, I also developed a friendship with HUSH, the writer who had beef with Tim. We never resolved their issues, but this didn't stop HUSH and I from developing a friendship based on our discussions of graffiti history, heavy theory, and politics. HUSH is a successful gallery artist, and much of his work is undergirded by a deep commitment to things mysterious and beautiful. He also is a serious political activist and has his hands in lot of different art and community projects.

I have fallen out of touch with the other writers in this study. AMAZE is in San Francisco, and I rarely see him anymore, but he has achieved his own amount of stardom. MEK and I had a falling out, but I hear these days he is healthy and sober.

Where these writers have drifted away new ones have taken their place as my graffiti teachers. Current writers like, ZER, KEZAM, and that dude who doesn't want me to mention his name keep me up to date and inspired.

To all the writers, past and future, thank you for your patience, tolerance, and everything that you've taught me. I am humbled by this culture and honored to have had the opportunity to tell some of your story.

Appendix

The New Ethnography

In its original form, ethnography involved close study of the native populations of exotic islands. These studies were an effort to understand "primitive man," and the results were utilized by colonial powers to better manage the people they ruled. Although today ethnography is no longer a tool of colonial control, the metaphor of colonists and natives still applies. Ethnographies are most often written by those in the academy about those who have less social, political, and cultural power. While this is not exactly the case for graffiti writers, some of whom have amassed a great deal of cultural and economic capital, I still was concerned about my inability to recognize my own privilege at work in our interactions. I wanted to make sure that I did not simplify graffiti culture into more manageable pieces by seeking to prove my own theory about the meaning of this cultural group. I needed a way to check myself and to allow others to do the same. In an effort toward highlighting and solving these problems, I created the blackbook to reflect the power differentials between these two cultural worlds.

Ethnography is essential to social science for its ability to uncover social data that is not readily available and to expand our knowledge of others and ourselves. But there is still the possibility that on some levels this research exploits those whom it studies. I will likely benefit more from this study than the people who shared their worlds with me, and so therefore I owe something to graffiti culture. Hopefully what I have written is a picture of graffiti culture that doesn't trivialize, simplify, or valorize, for the purpose of consumption or control, and instead illustrates complex cultural practices by people who are at least as complicated as we view ourselves to be.

There are numerous ethnographers across a range of disciplines who have inspired this commitment. In the last two decades, anthropologists, criminologists, and sociologists have become conscious of the way they impose representations onto other people's cultures. This awareness of how one's own position of privilege and power serves to construct the culture of others has led to a serious discussion and debate about how research is done and how ethnographies are written.

Many of the new ethnographies attempt to highlight the power relationships between authors and subjects in an effort to remove the discipline from its historical role as a tool of colonial rule.[1] Cultural anthropologists have utilized literary techniques to blur the strict positivist line between subject and object. Interpretive ethnographers have sought to explore the emotional space of human subjectivity. Cultural criminologists are similarly smudging the moral absolutes between author and criminal, legality and illegality.[2] In many of these works, the author no longer plays the role of omniscient narrator speaking for voiceless natives. Instead, ethnographers actively engage with others across social and emotional boundaries and make this experience part of the story. H. L. Goodall, who has been writing about writing ethnography for over twenty years, defines the "new" ethnography as "creative narratives shaped out of a writer's personal experiences within a culture and addressed to academic and public audiences."[3]

Some of these new forms of ethnography are presented in the 1996 book *Composing Ethnography*, edited by Carolyn Ellis and Arthur Bochner. They make a plea for the kind of ethnography that their series, called "Ethnographic Alternatives," is looking for:

> The editors encourage submissions that experiment with novel forms of expressing lived experience, including literary, poetic, autobiographical, multi-voiced, conversational, critical, visual, performative, and co-constructed representations. Emphasis should be on expressing concrete lived experience through narrative modes of writing.
>
> We are interested in ethnographic alternatives that promote narration of local stories, literary modes of descriptive scene setting, dialogue, and unfolding action; and inclusion of the author's subjective reactions, involvement in the research process, and strategies for practicing reflexive fieldwork.[4]

The essays in *Composing Ethnography* present powerful evocations of lived experience previously shrouded by patriarchy and science. The collection showcases scholars experimenting with what they call autoethnography, sociopoetics, and reflexive ethnography—terms chosen not for their descriptive clarity but as a "way of opening the discussion about alternative genres of ethnography."[5]

The Problem of Representation

In the introduction to the collection of essays published as *Writing Culture*, James Clifford questions the traditional notion of ethnographic representation. Clifford begins by focusing on the written nature of ethnographic texts, arguing that all writing, even scientific writing, to a certain degree holds to literary conventions, which include the use of metaphor, rhetoric, and style. Therefore, he claims, ethnographic writing is fiction, in the sense of something made. Ethnographers are potentially constructing culture as they report it.

Anthropologist John Langston Gwaltney shows what is at stake in the academic representation of others. In the introduction to his book *Drylongso: A Self-Portrait of Black America*, he writes, "The people whose voices are heard in these pages are eminently capable of self-expression and I have relied upon them to speak for themselves."[6] The author's voice remains in the background, giving only brief intros before letting each of his participants speak their piece. As members of a racially oppressed group, both Gwaltney and his informants have experienced numerous misrepresentations, and he is critical of the role that anthropology has played in the dissemination of racist myths of black folk.[7] The participants in *Drylongso* are also aware of the ways in which representation makes people vulnerable to exploitation. Gwaltney makes sure to include his respondents' continued admonitions for him to "get it right." His contacts express confidence that Gwaltney, whom they consider one of their own, will not make the same mistakes as other social scientists whose goal was the definitive representation of blackness. Making it absolutely clear what is at stake in the representation of others, and in recognition of the power of ethnography to exploit and express, he begins his text with an epigraph from Othman Sullivan, who says, "I think this anthropology is just another way to call me nigger." Gwaltney's book, however, shows how ethnography, when done right, can provide intimate knowledge of the quotidian experience of other people's lives.

Urban ethnography has its roots in the Chicago School, when sociologists there were shifting the focus away from macro-theoretical accounts and toward empirical studies of micro-social worlds. Robert Park quipped that "civilized man is just as interesting as primitive" and encouraged his students to utilize ethnographic methods to explore the city, which they used as a "laboratory for learning." However, urban sociologists have been relatively silent in these debates over self, culture, others, and representation. This is somewhat ironic because many of these folk are white scholars who have often done research with those of a different race, class, and gender, and have for the most part consistently gotten it right.[8]

Ethnographic Collaborations

For my book I took William Foote Whyte's *Street Corner Society* as a model. This detailed and fascinating study of "the corner boys," first published in 1947, holds up to modern scrutiny. Whyte was aware of his privileged social position and was concerned about being a "tourist" in the Italian slums. He chose to forgo his Harvard dormitory in favor of a room in the Martini family home in "Cornerville," where he ingratiated himself by trying to learn Italian.[9]

Rather than merely record the corner boys, Whyte discovered that Doc, for example, had a rich sociological imagination and even asked him to assist in the analysis of some of the data. On this subject Whyte writes, "Our time spent in this discussion of ideas and observations made Doc, in a very real sense, a collaborator in the research."[10] This shows one of the ways that actively crossing borders has the potential to combat structural inadequacies of the education system, as two people mentor each other in their respective fields. This occurs when observer and observed view each other as equals. Whyte highlights the fact that in close ethnographic relationships learning flows back and forth, rather than just away from the informant. This is greater than the simple psychological benefits of having someone listen to your stories. Doc experienced a new perspective on his own social world. At one point he told Whyte, "You've slowed me up plenty since you've been down here. Now when I do something, I have to think what Bill Whyte would want to know about it and how I can explain it. Before, I used to do things by instinct."[11]

In a recent work, sociologist Mitchell Duneier has continued this project of developing collaborative relationships with key informants. In *Sidewalk*, Hakim Hassan goes from selling books on the street to teaching college courses.[12] The unique thing about this book from a methodological perspective is that Hassan, a man well-versed in urban literature, collaborates in the research and then writes an afterword. This has the effect of problematizing the role of voice from the perspective of the subject.

Hassan asks and answers tough questions about the informant's role in the research process. He writes about his hesitation to allow himself to become Duneier's subject:

> How could I prevent him from appropriating me as mere data, from not giving me a voice in how the material in his book would be selected and depicted? How does a subject take part in an ethnographic study in which he has very little faith and survive as something more than a subject and less than an author?[13]

In this astounding work, Duneier treats his informant as a social and intellectual equal, which allows Hassan to become more than just subject. However, if not for the courage that Hassan displayed in critiquing the eminent sociologist's first draft, *Sidewalk* would have been a very different book. Yet, together they produced more than a book. From a political perspective, good ethnography tells stories but also can impact people's life chances. Duneier encouraged Hassan to return to the formal economy and invited him to co-teach an undergraduate seminar in Santa Barbara, and it is there that they began to realize the shortcomings of the original manuscript. They concluded that it was necessary to include the lives of the magazine vendors and the whole homeless population that revolved around the book-vending scene, access that was granted to Duneier with Hassan acting as his sponsor. Today Hassan works at a college and is himself a professional writer contemplating a career in the academy.

Techniques for Dismantling

Although *Body and Soul: Notebooks of an Apprentice Boxer* by Loïc Wacquant did not come out until late in this project, it achieved most of the goals I had set for myself and encouraged me to explore experimental techniques even further. *Body and Soul* is an urban autoethnography that shows the researcher in action, gives us a sense of his perspective, and evokes the scenes and rhythms of a boxing gym in Chicago. Wacquant refers to his method as "carnal sociology," and he uses his body, literally, as a punching bag to amass knowledge. His goal is to provide a descriptive, almost erotic, look at the act of boxing and the role the gym plays in the community. He feels the best way to accomplish this is to throw himself completely into the task of learning to box, a process he calls "initiatory immersion." Wacquant shirks old warnings about going native and instead proudly seeks to initiate himself into this warrior circle. The question of objectivity becomes moot. What he gains from trying to be accepted is firsthand knowledge of boxing and boxers.

While Wacquant uses his body to engage with others, some researchers have used techniques that inspire a performance of subcultural knowledge, what cultural criminologists call interactive devices.[14] I created the blackbook as a way of instigating graffiti writers to talk, both visually and verbally, about what they do and why they do it, and to help to translate some aspects of the culture into terms the larger society could understand. I wanted to encourage writers to show their talents in a safe and legal context. I wanted to create a forum where the issues and topics for discussion could be shaped by the writers, while forcing them to also be aware of a different and larger audience. I also adopted this technique because I thought that it would foster trust by showing that I was willing to listen.

I call this method "instigative reporting" because the researcher instigates informants to perform their culture in a different context. These strategies must be culturally specific to the group under study, and this requires some initial knowledge. This research becomes an experiment between researcher and informant, and both parties must be willing to risk losing control. No one knows what actually is going to happen.

Visual Sociology

Throughout this project I have been inspired by methods of visual sociology. Instigative reporting shares some elements with a process called "photo elicitation" first developed by John Collier in 1967 and perfected by Douglas Harper in his stunning book *Working Knowledge: Skill and Community in a Small Shop.*[15] In photo elicitation, the ethnographer photographs contacts doing various activities and then returns with the completed photos and asks questions about what the photos reveal. In this way the informant becomes the teacher, telling the researcher what the photos show. Many times, as Harper says in an essay on visual sociology, "a shocking thing happens in this interview format; the photographer who knows his or her photograph as its maker (often having slaved over its creation in the darkroom) suddenly confronts the realization that he or she knows little about the cultural information contained in the image."[16]

With my blackbook, the writer would take the book and call me when the artwork was completed to set up an interview. I would focus my questioning on why the writer chose the word they did, and I would get a lesson about many different aspects of graffiti as well as insights into a particular writer's interests, both personally and artistically.

There is a certain communion between the artist and the viewer that dismantles some of the hierarchies of the interview. Both methods provide for mutual learning and a back-and-forth flow of information. However, my method differs from photo elicitation in two significant ways. First, instigative reporting must be specific to the group under study. Second, the blackbook provided a foundation from which to begin a relationship. Unlike photo elicitation, where every interview has new photos for the informant to interpret, writers only did one "piece" in my blackbook. The blackbook was meant to inspire a relationship and to further my role as participant observer in varying degrees of proximity.

Terry Williams and William Kornblum were among the first to invent special techniques for collaborating with their contacts. For their book *The Uptown Kids*, they recruited young people to write in journals and meet in weekly sessions. This had the effect of engaging with young people without stripping them of their ability to speak for themselves. The Harlem Writers Crew, as they came to be known, also provided a space for learning. As crew members expressed themselves through their writing and taught the researchers about their lives, they were also encouraged to hone their writing skills.

In this way the ethnographic experience gives back some of what it takes. Much like the Writers Crew, Jim Hubbard created the Shooting Back organization in which he taught photography to homeless youth in Washington, D.C. In learning and honing a new skill, these kids found a freedom to express themselves and to share with the world a new vision of themselves. This project resulted in the book *Shooting Back: A Photographic View of Life by Homeless Youth*. Hubbard continued the Shooting Back project, reaching out to other "at-risk" youth. In *Shooting Back from the Reservation: A Photographic View of Life by Native American Youth*, Hubbard reached out to young Native Americans and taught them a skill that allowed them to express their own creativity and inspired an eagerness to learn not found in more traditional educational settings. Being asked to share with the world a view of the reservation from the perspective of the people who experience it is a powerful confidence builder for these young people and winds up having a huge impact on both the makers and the viewers of the photographs.

I believe that these strategies for learning from others unlike ourselves are helpful for dismantling relationships of power and crossing social boundaries. And yet it is also the case that sometimes people have difficulty articulating their culture because to them their world is normal. Posing interesting experiments with subculture participants acts as an educational tool for both researcher and subject. As my own method showed, these techniques help to break down some of the assumptions each has of the other. I made a book to discuss how a subculture based on names constructed new meanings for words. What the blackbook helped me to learn was that the meaning of words actually meant very little, as writers were more interested in the aesthetics of letters. I'm not sure how long I would have held onto my own theoretical position, or if I would have really listened to what writers were trying to tell me about letters, if the blackbook hadn't made it so abundantly clear that I was wrong. To this end I believe that experimental techniques like the one I utilized could be expanded in an effort to study subcultures, in a collaborative fashion, that seeks to minimize exploitation and maximize the exchange and creation of knowledge.

Throughout this project I was constantly aware of the differences between myself and the writers, but this difference inspired an incessant curiosity that eventually became a muse to knowledge. This is not the definitive telling of graffiti culture, but I hope that in some way this work contributes to numerous discussions about graffiti, youth, ethnography, crime, and career.

 Glossary

ALL-CITY A writer whose name is up all over the city. In New York this means tags, throw-ups, and pieces in all five boroughs.

BEEF Disputes, often caused by painting over (dissing) someone else's work.

BITE To copy another writer's style. n. Something unoriginal.

BLACKBOOK A writer's sketchbook, used to keep outlines and also autographs from other writers. Also called a PIECEBOOK.

BOMB To paint a name often in any form on many different surfaces.

BUFF To clean graffiti off of a surface with chemicals or by painting over it.

BUM RUSH To force your way into a situation in which you are not otherwise welcome.

BURNER A graffiti painting exhibiting intricate style and impressive use of color.

CAN CONTROL The ability to manipulate and control aerosol paint.

CHARACTER A graffiti figure, usually taken from comic books.

CIPHER A term used frequently in hip hop and rap lyrics; a small group of individuals sharing deep ideas, often used to connote a circle of rappers trading improvised lyrics.

CREW A group of writers who formally come together for camaraderie, to promote a style, and to insure physical protection.

DESIGNS Stars, arrows, halos, etc., used to add flavor to a piece, tag, or throw-up.

DIS/DISRESPECT To insult someone, or to paint over someone's graffiti.

DOWN LOW/D.L. Something secretive or hush-hush; information not to be passed on. This has recently taken on new meaning of engaging in secretive homosexual acts.

FALLING OFF Used to refer to a writer whose skills are diminishing or whose presence on the streets is waning.

FAME   What a writer gets when he or she is up consistently.

FAT CAPS   Tips for aerosol cans used to vary the width of the spray paint.

FILL-IN   The area inside the letters of a piece that is filled in with colors; also, another name for a throw-up.

FIVE-O OR **5-OH**   Cops. The term comes from the 1970s television show *Hawaii Five-O.*

FLICKS   Photographs of graffiti.

FREESTYLE   To rhyme or paint off the top of one's head without a preconceived plan; spontaneous improvisation.

FRONT/FRONTIN'   To act fake or put up a front; also, to dismiss something's importance

GEEKED   To be overly excited about something.

GET UP   To get your name up on any surface.

HAND SKILLS/HAND STYLE   A writer's penmanship, or ability to fight.

HERB   (pronounced without a silent "h," as in Herbert) Derogatory name for someone who is not cool.

KING   A term for a graffiti writer who is up the most in any given area; also, a general term for a highly talented and successful writer.

KRINK   Silver ink created and sold by KR that has become the industry standard.

LAY-UP   Underground holding area for out-of-service trains.

MAD   A lot of something, e.g., money or skills.

MASTER   An accomplished graffiti writer who has both style and ups, i.e., graffiti in the street.

MEAN STREAKS   Oil paint sticks that come in a multitude of colors and are used for tagging.

MISSION   Any long trip or journey to paint or to obtain supplies.

MOP   Emptied-out shoe polish bottle filled with industrial grade Marsh ink, used for tagging.

OUTLINE   A piece sketched on paper that may or may not be a template for a graffiti mural.

PERMISSION WALL/LEGAL WALL   A wall that a writer has obtained permission to piece.

PIECE   As a noun (short for "masterpiece"), a graffiti mural; as a verb, to draw or paint a masterpiece.

PIECEBOOK   A writer's sketchbook, used to keep outlines and also autographs from other writers. Also called a BLACKBOOK.

PRODUCTIONS   Murals (usually legal) done by a group of artists in a crew on a large surface.

PROPS   Proper respect.

RACK/RACKING   Stealing, shoplifting. The original term was "inventing."

SQUASH   To deal with a dispute diplomatically rather than through physical confrontation, as in "squashing a beef." Often initiated by an arbiter.

TAG   As a noun, a graffiti writer's signature; as a verb, to mark one's name on any surface.

THREE-D/3-D   Lines added to a piece to give the impression of depth.

THROW-UP   A name painted with two colors, an outline, and a fill-in color; also called a fill-in.

TOP TO BOTTOM   Originally, a graffiti painting that stretched from the top of the train to the bottom. Today it is used for any painting that fills the entire space.

TOY   A neophyte writer with no skills and little clue of the history of the culture.

TROOPER   A writer who puts in a lot of legwork and gets up all over the city.

UPS   The presence of one's graffiti in the street, e.g., "She has mad ups."

WILDSTYLE   Name given to any unreadable or fresh graffiti style. The origin of this term has a long and contested history, with TRACY 168 and PHASE II often being credited. *Wild Style* is also the name of graffiti's most famous film, which gave the term national and even worldwide currency.

WRITER'S BENCHES   Places such as the 149th Street subway station where writers would congregate to discuss the work on the trains.

VAMP   To approach younger writers, usually toys, and steal their paint.

PROLOGUE

1. It is a common practice in books and magazines on graffiti to put writers' names in capital letters, a convention I have followed in this book.

INTRODUCTION

1. Craig Castleman, *Getting Up: Subway Graffiti in New York* (Boston: MIT Press, 1982). At the time this book was out of print and listed as "missing" from most libraries in New York City.

2. Jeff Ferrell's *Crimes of Style: Urban Graffiti and the Politics of Criminality* (Boston: Northeastern University Press, 1993) was unavailable until it was reprinted in 1996, and focuses on graffiti in Denver, Colorado.

3. *Wild Style*, directed by Charlie Ahearn (1983). *Style Wars*, directed by Henry Chalfant and Tony Silver (1985). Norman Mailer, with text) photographs by Jon Naar and Mervyn Kurlansky, *The Faith of Graffiti* (New York: Praeger, 1974). Henry Chalfant and Martha Cooper, *Subway Art* (London: Thames and Hudson, 1985). Henry Chalfant and James Prigoff, *Spraycan Art* (London: Thames and Hudson, 1987).

4. Although I am no longer active in the field, I have maintained close friendships with VERT, ESPO, and AME.

5. Nancy Macdonald, *The Graffiti Subculture: Youth, Masculinity and Identity in London and New York* (London: Palgrave, 2001). Macdonald also talks about "reading the walls" (p. 55).

6. Castleman, *Getting Up*, p. 67. Ferrell, in *Crimes of Style*, p. 11, also notes this economic and racial diversity in the graffiti writing scene in Denver.

7. The global aspect of graffiti was first documented in Chalfant and Prigoff, *Spraycan Art*.

8. See Leroi Jones (a.k.a. Imamu Amira Baraka, *Blues People: Negro Music in White America* (New York: William Morrow, 1963). See also Bikari Kitwana, *Why White Kids Love Hip Hop: Wiggers, Wangstas and Wannabees* (New York: Basic Civitas Books, 2004).

9. Ferrell, *Crimes of Style*, p. 63.

10. I have heard this story numerous times. See also Chalfant and Silver, *Style Wars*, 20th anniversary edition; Dumar Brown, *NOV York: Written by a Slave* (New York: Xlibris, 2002), p. 37, where he describes how easy it is for white kids to steal paint, which they would then share with fellow writers of color.

11. On Amadou Diallo, see www.amadoudiallofoundation.org.

12. Ron K. Brunson, "Police Don't Like Black People: African-American Young Men's Accumulated Police Experiences," *Criminology and Public Policy* 6, no. 1 (February 2007).

13. See also www.at149st.com/women.html for a list a female writers.

14. See Angela Ashman, "Claw Money Honey: A Legendary Graffiti Artist Turned Fashion Designer Cashes in Her Street Cred," *Village Voice*, March 6, 2007.

15. See www.clawmoney.com.

16. James Q. Wilson and George Kelling, "Broken Windows: Police and Neighborhood Safety," *Atlantic Monthly*, March 1982, pp. 29–38.

17. Jeff Ferrell, *Tearing Down the Streets: Adventures in Urban Anarchy* (New York: Palgrave, 2001), p. 228.

18. Bernard Harcourt and Jens Ludwig, "Reefer Madness: Broken Windows Policing and Misdemeanor Marijuana Arrests in New York City, 1989–2000," *Criminology and Public Policy* 6, no.1 (February 2007).

19. Joe Austin, *Taking the Train: How Graffiti Art Became an Urban Crisis in New York City* (New York, Columbia University Press, 2001).

20. Thomas Lueck, "Graffiti Back in the Subways, Indelibly This Time," *New York Times*, April 25.

21. See www.nyc.gov/html/tlc/downloads/pdf/transcript_07_26_05.pdf, pp. 14–15. See also Tony Sclafani, "NYPD Can Do War vs. Graffiti," *Daily News*, November 14, 2005.

22. Jack Katz, *Seductions of Crime: A Chilling Exploration of the Criminal Mind—From Juvenile Delinquency to Cold-Blooded Murder* (New York: Basic Books, 1988). See also Ferrell, *Crimes of Style*; idem., *Tearing Down the Streets*; and Jeff Ferrell et al., eds., *Cultural Criminology Unleashed* (London: Glasshouse Press, 2004).

23. A recent example would be the *Graffiti: New Gifts* exhibition at the Brooklyn Museum, September 2006.

24. See also the National Public Radio series *This American Life* with Ira Glass, Episode 309, Cat and Mouse, Act 4, "Spray My Name, Spray My Name," Brian Thomas Gallagher reporting, original air date, February 24, 2006.

25. For more on graffiti magazines, see the section below titled "Over the Wall: Graffiti Media and Creating a Career."

26. Graffiti writers use photo sites such as Flickr.com to showcase their work The first and most comprehensive graffiti website is "Art Crimes." www.graffiti.org.

27. See Tricia Rose, *Black Noise: Rap Music and Black Culture* (Middletown, CT: Wesleyan University Press, 1994); D. Brewer and M. Miller, "Bombing and Burning: The Social Organization and Values of Hip Hop Graffiti Writers and Implications for Policy," *Deviant Behavior* 11 (1990); I. Miller, *Aerosol Kingdom: Subway Painters of New York City* (Jackson: University Press of Mississippi, 2002); M. Walsh, *Graffito* (San Francisco: North Atlantic Books, 1996).

28. R. Lachmann, "Graffiti as Career and Ideology," *American Journal of Sociology* 94, no. 2 (1988).

29. See www.Tatscru.com, www.clawmoney.com, and www.krink.com. On former writers who are now professional journalists, see Jessica Pressler, "Remember Zines? Look at Them Now," *New York Times*, May 7, 2006, sec. 9, p. 14.

30. See chapters 19–22.

1 Getting In

STARTING THE BLACKBOOK

1. See, e.g., W. E. B. Du Bois, *The Souls of Black Folk* (1903; reprint, New York: Signet, 1969); R. Kelley, *Yo Mama's Dysfunctional: Fighting the Culture Wars in Urban America* (New York: Beacon Press, 1997); Cornel West, *Race Matters* (New York: Vintage Books, 1994); bell hooks, *Yearning: Race, Gender and Cultural Politics* (Boston: South End Press, 1990); C. Ellis and A. Bochner, *Composing Ethnography: Alternative Forms of Qualitative Research* (Walnut Creek, CA: AltaMira Press, 1996); N. Denzin, *Interpretive Ethnography: Ethnographic Practices for the 21st Century* (Thousand Oaks, CA: Sage, 1997).

2. T. Williams and W. Kornblum, *The Uptown Kids: Struggle and Hope in the Projects* (New York: G. P. Putnam and Sons, 1994).

3. The Harlem Writers Crew spawned a movie, *Harlem Diaries*, as well as The Harlem Writers Crew Foundation.

4. See Ned Polsky, *Hustlers, Beats, and Others* (New York, Anchor Books, 1969), p. 119; Ferrell et al., *Cultural Criminology Unleashed*; J. Ferrell and M. Hamm, eds., *Ethnography at the Edge* (Boston: Northeastern University Press, 1998).

5. Douglas Harper, "On the Authority of the Image: Visual Methods at the Crossroads," in *Handbook of Qualitative Research*, ed. Norman K. Denzin and Yvonna S. Lincoln (Thousand Oaks, CA: Sage, 1994).

6. For example, ESPO and I were both born in 1968.

7. See Stephen Powers, *The Art of Getting Over: Graffiti at the Millennium* (New York: St. Martin's Press, 1999); Andrew Witten and Michael White, *Dondi White: Style Master General* (New York: Regan Books, 2001); Peter Sutherland, *Autograf: New York City's Graffiti Writers* (New York: Powerhouse Books, 2004).

8. See H. Becker, *Outsiders: Studies in the Sociology of Deviance* (New York: Free Press, 1963); Lachmann, "Graffiti as Career and Ideology."

9. Stuart Hall and Tony Jefferson, eds., *Resistance through Rituals: Youth Subcultures in Postwar Britain* (London: Hutchinson, 1976).

10. Susan Krieger, *Social Science and the Self: Personal Essays on an Artform* (New Brunswick, NJ: Rutgers University Press, 1991).

11. Gregory Snyder, "The Danced Conversion: Dance and African Cultural Continuity in the Christianization of American Slaves," unpublished MA thesis, New School for Social Research, 1997.

12. D. Reed-Danahay, ed., *Auto/Ethnography: Rewriting the Self and the Social* (New York: Berg, 1997); Ellis and Bochner, *Composing Ethnography*.

13. George Marcus, *Ethnography through Thick and Thin* (Princeton: Princeton University Press, 1998), p. 15.

14. John Van Maanen, *Tales of the Field: On Writing Ethnography* (Chicago: University of Chicago Press, 1988), p. 133. See also Adam Begley, "The I's Have It," *Lingua Franca* 4 (1994): 54–59.

15. See Denzin, *Interpretive Ethnography*.

16. On homelessness, for example, one can read both Mitch Duneier's *Sidewalk* (New York: Farrar Straus and Giroux, 1999) and Lee Stringer's *Grand Central Winter* (New York: Seven Stories Press, 1998), which describes his transition from homeless crack addict to successful writer. See also the autobiographical novel *NOV York: Written by a Slave* (New York: Xlibris, 2002), by graffiti writer NOV, a.k.a. Dumar Brown, as well as the self-published book from downtown artist Livingroom Johnston *I Don't Want to Think about It Right Now* (Brooklyn, NY: Magic Propaganda Press, 2005).

A BRIEF HISTORY OF GRAFFITI WRITING

1. See www.subwayoutlaws.com for a fairly detailed history of the beginnings of the writing movement.

2. See Powers, *The Art of Getting Over*, p. 10. There is also a movie based roughly on CORNBREAD's life, called *Cornbread, Earl and Me* (1975), starring Lawrence Fishburn and directed by Joseph Manduke.

3. Herbert Kohl, "Names, Graffiti and Culture," in *Rappin' and Stylin' Out*, ed. T. Kochman (Urbana: University of Illinois Press, 1972).

4. For the early history of New York subway graffiti, see Jack Stewart, "Subway Graffiti: An Aesthetic Study of Graffiti on the Subway System of New York City, 1970–1978." Ph.D. diss., New York University, 1989.

5. Castleman, *Getting Up*, p. 55.

6. PHASE II is generally credited with inventing the cloud style.

7. Castleman, *Getting Up*, p. 26. Castleman also has a good discussion of the contributions of these early writers on pp. 52–60.

8. Many people assume that graffiti writers and writing were generally disliked by the public; however, Joe Austin's close reading of op-eds and letters to the editor and numerous pieces by Richard Goldstein of the *Village Voice* contradict this notion. See Joe Austin, "Knowing Their Place: Local Knowledge, Social Prestige, and the Writing Formation in New York City," in *Generations of Youth: Youth Cultures and History in Twentieth-Century America*, ed. J. Austin and M. Willard (New York: New York University Press, 1998); see also the articles by Goldstein listed in the bibliography below.

9. Austin, "Knowing Their Place," p. 147 (emphasis in original).

10. Richard Goldstein, "In Praise of Graffiti, The Fire Down Below," *Village Voice*, December 24–30, 1980.

11. It would be wrong to assume that writers who were inspired by books or films rather than New York trains are somehow less authentic. Writers who show skills are given respect, regardless of their point of entry into the culture.

12. For more on the early phases of the gallery scene, see Witten and White, *Dondi White*, pp. 146–80.

13. *Elementary Magazine*, no. 1 (1996).

14. *Mass Appeal Magazine*, no. 7 (1999).

15. See the "Hand of Doom" and "Children of the Grave" subway pieces in Cooper and Chalfant, *Subway Art*, pp. 56–57 and 68–69.

16. On hip hop, see Rose, *Black Noise*; Neal 2004.

17. *On the Go*, April 1996.

18. For a passionate discussion of this, see David Schmidlapp and Phase 2, *Style: Writing from the Underground* (Terni, Italy: Stampa Alternativa, 1996).

19. This issue is complex and might simply come down to region and ethnicity. Placas date back to the early 1950s in East Los Angeles's Mexican barrios, while the graffiti tradition comes from New York City. Charles "CHAZ" Bojorquez is a graffiti writer well-versed in these traditions.

20. Brewer and Miller, "Bombing and Burning," p. 354.

21. Zulu Nation was the organization begun by DJ Afrika Bambaataa to promote peace and hip hop.

22. Again, this is not a claim about race. New York's punk scene included black and white kids. Nor is it a code, as in the case of rock vs. disco, or a claim to try and whiten graffiti's historical legacy. These are the facts of graffiti and the hip hop movement.

23. Ferrell, *Crimes of Style*, p. 7.

24. Susan Phillips, *Wallbangin': Graffiti and Gangs in L.A.* (Chicago: University of Chicago Press, 1999), p. 22.

25. See Jeff Ferrell and Clinton R. Sanders, *Cultural Criminology* (Boston: Northeastern University Press, 1995); Ferrell et al., eds., *Cultural Criminology Unleashed*; Jeff Ferrell, *Tearing Down the Streets: Adventures in Urban Anarchy* (New York: Palgrave, 2001).

26. On freight train graffiti, see Jeff Ferrell, "Freight Train Graffiti: Subculture, Crime, Dislocation," *Justice Quarterly* 15, no. 4 (1998): 587–608; Roger Gastman, Darin Rowland, and Ian Sattler, *Freight Train Graffiti*(New York, Harry N. Abrams, 2006).

27. This was confirmed by JA on a recent WNYU radio program, "The Halftime Show."

28. See Ferrell, *Crimes of Style*, chap. 2, for a similar description.

29. TRACY 168 is credited with inventing the term "wildstyle." See Jamie Bryan, "Ganja Graffiti," *High Times Magazine*, August 1996, pp. 52–62.

30. Today's writers have access to a wider range of skinny and fat caps that are produced by European companies specifically for writers.

31. See the section below on "Legal Graffiti."

32. For a detailed description of an underground mission with REVS, see Powers, *The Art of Getting Over*, p. 94.

33. Espoet, a.k.a. Steve Powers, *On the Go Magazine*, no. 10 (1995).

34. This is confirmed in Castleman, *Getting Up*, pp. 57–61. The idea that the throw-up is the mass production of the name and T.O.P. crew's role in this comes from conversations with HUSH.

35. Today, many writers use KRink, an indelible ink developed by KR, who sponsors many writers by providing them with free supplies.

36. For an excellent photo essay of writers' tools, see Angela Boatwright in *Mass Appeal Magazine*, no. 9, pp. 11–18.

37. The lesson in Philly styles comes from conversations with DES.

38. For more on this see, Charles "CHAZ" Bojorquez, "Los Angelos 'Cholo' Style Graffiti Art," http://www.graffitiverite.com/cb-cholowriting.htm.

39. On corporate advertisers' use of graffiti, see Heitor Alvelos, "The Desert of Imagination in the City of Signs: Cultural Implications of Sponsored Transgression and Branded Graffiti," in Ferrell et al., *Cultural Criminology Unleashed*. See also sneakers by NECKFACE, ESPO, and COPE, as well as the videogame *Getting Up*, designed by former graffiti writer turned fashion mogul Mark Ecko.

40. Jerald G. Bachman et al., *The Decline of Substance Use in Adulthood* (Mahwah, NJ: Lawrence Erlbaum Associates, 2001). J. Arnett, "Young People's Conceptions of the Transition to Adulthood," *Youth and Society* 29 (1997): 3–23.

41. F. Furstenburg et al., "Becoming an Adult: The Changing Nature of Early Adulthood," *Contexts* 3 (2004): 33–41; D. Hoganand N. Astone, "The Transition to Adulthood," *Annual Review of Sociology* 12 (1986): 109–30.

42. Ferrell, *Crimes of Style*; Jeff Ferrell, "Style Matters: Criminal Identity and Social Control," in *Cultural Criminology*, ed. Ferrell and Sanders; Jeff Ferrell,

"Urban Graffiti: Crime, Control, and Resistance," *Youth and Society* 27, no. 1 (September 1995).

43. C. Uggen, "Work as a Turning Point in the Life Course of Criminals: A Duration Model of Age, Employment, and Recidivism," *American Sociological Review* 65 (2000): 529–46; C. Uggen and S. Wakefield, "Young Adults Reentering the Community from the Criminal Justice System: Challenges to Adulthood," in *On Your Own Without a Net: The Transition to Adulthood for Vulnerable Populations*, ed. D. W. Osgood et al. (Chicago: University of Chicago Press).

CRIME SPACE VS. COOL SPACE: BREAKING DOWN BROKEN WINDOWS

1. Wilson and Kelling, "Broken Windows."
2. Harcourt and Ludwig, "Reefer Madness".
3. Jeffrey Fagan and Fritz Davis, "Street Stops and Broken Windows: Terry, Race and Disorder in New York City," *Fordham Urban Law Journal* 28 (2000): 457.
4. A. Karmen, *New York Murder Mystery: The True Story behind the Crime Crash of the 1990s* (New York: New York University Press, 2000.

② GETTING UP

VERT: FIRST CONTACT

1. See the 2006 film *American Hardcore: A History of American Punk 1980–1986*, directed by Paul Rachman.
2. Pierre Bordieu, *Distinction: A Social Critique of the Judgment of Taste* (Cambridge: Harvard University Press, 1984); Sarah Thornton, *Club Cultures: Music, Media and Subcultural Capital* (Hanover, NH: Wesleyan University Press, 1996).
3. "Mosh" is the typical dance in a hardcore "pit," while break dancing is associated with hip hop.
4. Martin Sanchez Jankowski, *Islands in the Street: Gangs and American Urban Society* (Berkeley: University of California Press, 1991).
5. Macdonald's *The Graffiti Subculture* focuses on graffiti as a site for the construction of male identity but spends very little time talking about beef and violence.
6. Powers confirms this in *The Art of Getting Over*, p. 106.
7. This spot has had many names: Soho Zat, Soho Down and Under, Bomb the System, and, currently, the Scrapyard.
8. Today all of the information contained in the magazines and videos can be found on the web in a matter of seconds.

9. The halo over the name was originally done by STAY HIGH 149, who co-opted the stick figure from the television show *The Saint* and drew a saint smoking a joint next to his tag. See also Schmidlapp and Phase 2, *Style*, p. 30.

10. See Ferrell and Hamm, eds., *Ethnography at the Edge*. "For the dedicated researcher who seeks to explore criminal subcultures . . . obeying the law may present as much of a problem as breaking it" (p. 26).

WRITER'S BLOCK: BLACKBOOK IN THE STREETS

1. A DVD of all the early Videograf's is currently available at www.graffitivideos.com.

2. See B. Berger, "On the Youthfulness of Youth Cultures," in *Youth and Sociology*, ed. Peter K. Manning and Marcello Truzzi (Englewood Cliffs, NJ: Prentice-Hall, 1972).

3. See the section on methodology above.

4. Despite their stated enthusiasm for graffiti, I never saw their names in public and their writing careers were short-lived.

5. Although I did not know it at the time, it is obvious to any established writer that CLIF and TESAA are toys—young writers putting on airs with no conception of the culture's history. CLIF had no clue that his name was taken from CLIFF, a legendary 1970s writer.

6. Check www.handselecta.com.

7. Ferrell has a similar account of the way tags tell stories. See *Crimes of Style*, p. 73.

8. Nearly ten years later UFO is still writing the same spaceship, but today he is a star. See Sutherland, *Autograf*.

9. Michelle de Certeau, *The Practice of Everyday Life* (Berkeley: University of California Press, 1984), p. 102; Henri Lefebvre, *The Production of Space* (London: Wiley, 1974; M. Gottdiener, *The Social Production of Urban Space* (Austin: University of Texas Press, 1985). For an excellent analysis of how skateboarders are realizing some of the spatial practices, see Iain Borden, *Skateboarding, Space and the City: Architecture and the Body* (London: Berg, 2001).

WELCOME TO ESPO LAND

1. Years later ESPO would take the initiative to repaint the signs on the Coney Island boardwalk, curating The Dreamland Artist Club and opening the Surf Avenue Sign Shop.

2. Now that ESPO is no longer an active graffiti writer he has become a paragon of fashion.

3. I have chosen not to reveal the names of the writers involved in order not to bring up old drama.

INTO THE TUNNEL: UNDER MANHATTAN

1. Jack Katz, *Seductions of Crime* (New York: Basic Books, 1988), p. 52.

2. Jennifer Toth, *The Mole People: Life in the Tunnels beneath New York City* (Chicago: Chicago Review Press, 1993), pp. 97–118; M. Morton, *The Tunnel* (New Haven: Yale University Press, 1995).

3. Bernard also plays a crucial role in Toth's *The Mole People*; see chap. 11.

4. On FREEDOM and his tunnel art, see ibid., chaps. 12 and 13.

A PILGRIMAGE TO MEK: A BRONX GRAFFITI TOUR

1. MEK, interview with the author, June 11, 1996.

2. Rose, *Black Noise*.

3. In graffiti lore, a "raid story" is a tale of how writers escaped the cops.

4. Cutting and scratching are techniques whereby DJs play a record and turntable like an instrument. Today this is also called "turntablism" to distinguish it from DJs who simply play records.

LEGAL GRAFFITI: CONTEMPORARY PERMISSION SPOTS

1. Castleman, *Getting Up*, pp. 117–25. Martinez is still involved in writing culture and operates a gallery that focuses on Puerto Rican graffiti art.

2. Chalfant and Prigoff, *Spraycan Art*, p. 24.

3. Ferrell, *Crimes of Style*, p. 39.

4. See Streets Are Saying Things at www.saster.net. This site calls itself the original online graffiti museum.

5. KEZAM, email to author, September 12, 2006.

6. The details about TATS CRU are from www.tatscru.com.

7. See www.altterrain.com.

8. Pat Delillo, interview with Joe Austin and the author, circa 1996.

9. See http://queens.about.com/od/thingtodo/ss/lic_art_2.htm.

STYLE POINTS: ESPO'S BROOKLYN MURAL

1. Powers, *The Art of Getting Over*, p. 39.

2. This would turn out to be a case of art imitating life: In early 2000, the cops came to ESPO's house and busted him. See the section "Grate Graffiti Solution" below.

3. Although there have been no definitive studies on the effects of spray paint on aerosol artists, studies have shown lower birth weights and pulmonary conditions in those who experience long-term exposure to commercial spray paint. See GuoBing Xiao et al., "Effect of Benzene, Toluene, Xylene on the Semen Quality and the Function of Accessory Gonad of Exposed Workers," *Industrial Health* 39 (2001): 206–10.

4. For an extremely detailed and esoteric account of the various caps and their uses, see http://www.a2planet.com/guide/.

5. Ferrell has also tried his hand at aerosol art.

AME: BOMBING STYLES, INVENTING SELF

1. See Katz, *Seductions of Crime*, chap. 3, "Ways of the Bad Ass."

2. Ariel Levy, "Chasing Dash Snow," *New York Magazine*, January 15, 2007. See also the documentary film *Infamy*, directed by Doug Pray (2006).

AMAZE: OUT OF TOWNER GETS UP IN THE TUNNEL

1. A claddagh ring is the traditional Irish wedding ring with two hands holding a heart.

2. AMAZE was one of the first writers to be "sponsored" by KR, who now supplies stars like EARSNOT with ink.

THE GRATE GRAFFITI SOLUTION: ESPO'S PUBLIC SERVICE ANNOUNCEMENT

1. N. Siegel, "From the Subways to the Streets," *New York Times*, August 22, 1999.

2. See Powers, *The Art of Getting Over*, pp. 78–79.

3. R. Goldstein, "Rudy's Most Wanted," *Village Voice*, December 15–22, 1999.

4. Steve Powers, email to the author, 2003.

③ GETTING OUT

OVER THE WALL: GRAFFITI MEDIA AND CREATING A CAREER

1. The practice of documenting feats and producing magazines and videos to share with others occurs across numerous subcultures, including skateboarding, snowboarding, street racing, and BASE jumping; see, e.g., J. Ferrell, D. Milovanovic, and S. Lyng, "Edgework, Media Practices, and the Elongation of Meaning," *Theoretical Criminology* 5, no. 2 (2001): 177–202.

2. The Art Crimes website (www.graffiti.org) has reviews of nearly two hundred graffiti magazines

3. Schmidlapp and Phase 2, *Style*, p. 45.

4. On the experience of legends like DONDI, FUTURA, LEE, BLADE, and others in U.S. and European galleries, see Witten and White, *Dondi White*, pp. 146–177.

5. Both *Wildstyle* and *Style Wars* have recently released twentieth anniversary DVDs.

6. In the early 1980s a group in New York that called themselves the Photo Kings encouraged the trading of flicks with kids in other cities. ESPO, interview with the author, 1996.

7. *VideoGraf* by Carl Weston and friends was the first graffiti video done in New York. See www.graffitivideos.com.

8. Becker, *Outsiders*.

9. Local politicians' "tough on graffiti" stance followed a similar path to that of late 1980s "tough on crime" politicians, who used such rhetoric to scare suburban voters into electing leaders to deal with "urban" problems. See C. Parenti, *Lockdown America: Police and Prisons in an Age of Crisis* (New York: Verso, 1996).

10. See Ferrell, and Austin.

11. ESPO, interview with the author, summer 1997.

12. Greil Marcus, *Lipstick Traces: A Secret History of the 20th Century* (Cambridge: Harvard University Press, 1990).

13. Stephen Duncombe, *Notes from Underground: Zines and the Politics of Alternative Culture* (New York: Verso, 1997).

14. Chris Atton, *Alternative Media* (London: Sage Press, 2002).

15. P. Hodkinson, *Goth: Identity, Style and Subculture* (Oxford: Berg, 2002).

16. See Alvelos, "The Desert of Imagination."

17. Jessica Pressler, "Remember 'Zines? Look at Them Now," *New York Times*, May 7, 2006.

WRITING STYLE: IT'S NOT WHAT YOU WEAR

1. D. Muggleton and R. Weinzierl, eds., *The Post-Subcultures Reader* (Oxford: Berg, 2003).

2. Albert Cohen, *Delinquent Boys: The Culture of the Gang* (New York: Free Press, 1955); R. Cloward and L. Ohlin, *Delinquency and Opportunity: A Theory of Delinquent Gangs* (New York: Free Press, 1961).

3. Becker, *Outsiders*.

4. On youth as a generation responsible for updating the values of the parent culture, see T. Parsons, "Youth in the Context of American Society," in *Social Structure and Personality* (New York: Free Press, 1963), chap. 7.

5. Stuart Hall and Tony Jefferson, eds., *Resistance through Rituals: Youth Subcultures in Post-War Britain*, 2d ed. (London: Routledge, 2007).

6. Claude Levi-Strauss, *Myth and Meaning* (New York: Schocken Books, 1979).

7. See Borden, *Skateboarding, Space and the City*.

8. See *On the Go* magazine, no. 11.

9. See the album artwork for *Follow the Leader*. On the Brooklyn Lo-Lifes, see www.myspace.com/lolifes1988. On shoplifting, see also Robert Weide, "eRacking: New Opportunities in the World of Professional Shoplifting" paper presented at the *On the Edge: Transgression and the Dangerous Other* conference, John Jay College, August 2007.

10. See Stanley Cohen, "Symbols of Trouble"; Angela McRobbie, "Second-Hand Dresses and the Role of the Ragmarket"; and Sarah Thornton, "The Social Logic of Subcultural Capital"; all in *The Subcultures Reader*, ed. Ken Gelder and Sarah Thornton (London: Routledge, 1997).

11. Dick Hebdige, *Subculture: The Meaning of Style* (London: Routledge, 1979).

12. David Muggleton, *Inside Subculture: The Postmodern Meaning of Style* (London: Berg, 2000), p. 2 (emphasis in original).

13. Hodkinson, *Goth*; Redhead, S. 1990, 1993, 1995, 1997. Muggleton, *Inside Subculture*; Thornton, 1994, 1995. Weinzierl, 2000.

14. See Austin and Willard, eds., Generations of Youth; A. Ross and T. Rose, eds., *Microphone Fiends: Youth Music and Youth Culture* (New York: Routledge, 1994).

15. Muggleton, *Inside Subculture*, p. 3.

16. Ferrell and Sanders, *Cultural Criminology*; Ferrell et al., eds., (2005) *Cultural Criminology Unleashed*; Keith Hayward, *City Limits: Crime, Consumer Culture and the Urban Experience* (London: Glasshouse Press, 2004).

17. This is certainly not the only example of subcultures that interest criminologists. See Ferrell, *Tearing Down the Streets*.

18. Katz, *Seductions of Crime*.

19. Ferrell, *Crimes of Style*; Ferrell, "Style Matters"; Jeff Ferrell, "Urban Graffiti: Crime, Control, and Resistance," *Youth and Society* 27, no. 1 (September 1995).

20. Uggen, "Work as a Turning Point," 529–46; Uggen and Wakefield, "Young Adults Reentering the Community."

21. Thornton uses "taste cultures" and "club cultures" to describe the rave scene, while the terms "tribes" and "neo-tribes" come from M. Maffesoli, *The Times of the Tribes: The Decline of Individualism in Mass Society* (London, Sage, 1996).

22. While those who know other writers may be more likely to write themselves, many writers are loners who begin on their own, inspired simply by what they see on walls.

23. This insight came about through a series of prodding questions from Tony Jefferson at the *On the Edge: Transgression and the Dangerous Other* conference, John Jay College, August 2007.

24. See Jeff Ferrell's extensive accounting of criminology texts that use photos of graffiti but make no mention of the culture itself in *Cultural Criminology: An Invitation*, ed. J. Ferrell, K. Hayward, and J. Young (London: Sage, forthcoming).

25. On contemporary youth's obsession with corporate style, see K. Hayward and M. Yar, "The 'Chav' Phenomenon: Consumption, Media and the Construction of a New Underclass," *Crime, Media, Culture* 2, no. 1 (2006).

26. Hall and Jefferson, eds., *Resistance through Rituals*, p. 47.

CAREER OPPORTUNITIES: RE-WRITING SUBCULTURE RESISTANCE

1. Becker, *Outsiders*, p. 30.

2. Ibid., p. 101.

3. Ibid., p. 111.

4. Lachmann, "Graffiti as Career and Ideology," pp. 229–50.

5. Howard Becker, *Art Worlds* (Berkeley: University of California Press, 1982).

6. While this was generally true of earlier graffiti generations, some writers are self-described loners who were inspired by the tags and pieces on walls and subways and just started writing.

7. Becker, *Art Worlds*, p. 71.

8. See also Castleman, *Getting Up*, pp. 110–11.

9. Lachmann, "Graffiti as Career and Ideology," p. 246.

10. This community has been reformed in virtual space, see www.@149th.com.

11. Lachmann, "Graffiti as Career and Ideology," p. 248. While it may be correct that none of Lachmann's contacts returned to street or gallery graffiti, many of the early gallery greats such as LEE, FUTURA, BLADE, and DONDI have never stopped being street and gallery graffiti artists, although their street work obviously decreased with age and success.

12. A. Rose and C. Strike, eds., *Beautiful Losers: Contemporary Art and Street Culture* (New York, Iconoclast Press, 2004).

13. Kelley, *Yo Mama's Dysfunctional*.

14. See also Witten and White, *Dondi White*.

15. "Beyond the vapors" is borrowed from a PHASE II article in *Rappages*, 1996.

TIMMY TATTOO: TIMMY'S LONG ISLAND TATTOO SHOP

1. At the time NYU Press had my manuscript and I was hoping like crazy they would offer me a contract.

GABE BANNER: MARKET WISE

1. Gabe Banner, interview with the author, summer 2006.

2. See also Roger Gastman, *Free Agents: A History of Washington, D.C. Graffiti* (Bethesda, MD: R. Rock Enterprises, 2001).

ESPO/STEVE POWERS: DREAM LAND ARTISTS CLUB

1. Rob Walker, "Slicker Price," *New York Times*, October 30, 2005.

2. Evan Pricco, *Juxtapose Magazine*, no. 83 (December 2007).

APPENDIX

1. See Ruth Behar, *The Vulnerable Observer: Ethnography That Breaks Your Heart* (Boston: Beacon Press, 1996).

2. See J. Clifford and G. Marcus, eds., *Writing Culture: The Poetics and Politics of Ethnography* (Berkeley: University of California Press, 1986); Norman K. Denzin and Yvonna S. Lincoln *Handbook of Qualitative Research* (Thousand Oaks, CA: Sage, 1994); C. Ellis and M. Flaherty, eds., *Investigating Subjectivity: Research on Lived Experience* (Newbury Park, CA: Sage, 1992); Ellis and Bochner, *Composing Ethnography*; Ferrell and Hamm, *Ethnography at the Edge*.

3. H. L. Goodall, *Writing the New Ethnography* (Walnut Creek, CA: AltaMira Press, 2000), p. 9.

4. Ellis and Bochner, *Composing Ethnography*.

5. Ibid., p. 1.

6. J. L. Gwaltney, *Drylongso: A Self-Portrait of Black America* (New York: New Press, 1980), p. xxii.

7. For a fierce critique of (white) anthropological constructions of the (black) ghetto, see Robin Kelley, "Looking for the Real Nigga: Social Scientists Construct the Ghetto," in Kelley, *Yo Mama's Dysfunctional*.

8. Jay MacLeod, *Ain't No Makin' It: Aspirations and Attainment in a Low-Income Neighborhood* (Boulder, CO: Westview Press, 1995); Dan Rose, *Black American Street Life: South Philadelphia, 1969-1971* (Philadelphia: University of Pennsylvania Press, 1987); Carol Stack, *All our Kin: Strategies for Survival in a Black Community* (New York: Harper and Row, 1974); William Foote Whyte, *Street Corner Society* (1947; reprint, Chicago: University of Chicago Press, 1973).

9. Whyte, *Street Corner Society*, p. 301.

10. Ibid.

11. Ibid.

12. Duneier, *Sidewalk*.

13. Ibid., p. 321.

14. Ferrell and Hamm, *Ethnography at the Edge*.

15. Douglas Harper, *Working Knowledge: Skill and Community in a Small Shop* (Chicago: University of Chicago Press, 1987).

16. Douglas Harper, "On the Authority of the Image: Visual Methods at the Crossroads," in *Handbook of Qualitative Research*, ed. Denzin and Lincoln.

BIBLIOGRAPHY

BOOKS AND ARTICLES

Alvelos, H. (2004). "The Desert of Imagination in the City of Signs: Cultural Implications of Sponsored Transgression and Branded Graffiti." In *Cultural Criminology Unleashed*, ed. J. Ferrell et al., pp. 181–91. London: Glasshouse Press.

Amit-Talai, V., and H. Wulff, eds. (1995). *Youth Cultures: A Cross-Cultural Perspective*. New York: Routledge.

Anderson, E. (1999). *Code of the Streets*. New York: W. W. Norton.

——— (1990). *Street Wise: Race, Class, and Change in an Urban Community*. Chicago: University of Chicago Press.

Arnett, J. (1997). "Young People's Conceptions of the Transition to Adulthood." *Youth and Society* 29:3–23.

Ashman, A. (2007) "Claw Money Honey: A Legendary Graffiti Artist Turned Fashion Designer Cashes in Her Street Credit." *Village Voice*, March 6.

Atton, C. (2002). *Alternative Media*. London: Sage.

Austin, J. (2001). *Taking the Train*. New York: Columbia University Press.

Austin, J., and M. Willard, eds. (1998). *Generations of Youth: Youth Cultures and History in Twentieth-Century America*. New York: New York University Press.

Becker, H. (1963). *Outsiders: Studies in the Sociology of Deviance*. New York: Free Press.

——— (1982). *Art Worlds*. Berkeley: University of California Press.

——— (1996). *Tricks of the Trade: How to Think about Your Research While You're Doing It*. Chicago: University of Chicago Press.

Behar, R. (1996). *The Vulnerable Observer: Anthropology That Breaks Your Heart*. Boston: Beacon Press.

Berger, B. (1971). *Looking for America: Essays on Youth, Suburbia and Other American Obsessions*. Englewood Cliffs, NJ: Prentice-Hall.

——— (1972). "On the Youthfulness of Youth Cultures." In *Youth and Sociology*, ed. Peter K. Manning and Marcello Truzzi. Englewood Cliffs, NJ: Prentice-Hall.

Borden, I. (2001). *Skateboarding, Space and the City: Architecture and the Body.* London: Berg.

Bordieu, P. (1984). *Distinction: A Social Critique of the Judgment of Taste.* Cambridge: Harvard University Press.

Bourgois, P. (1995). *In Search of Respect: Selling Crack in El Barrio.* New York: Cambridge University Press.

Brake, M. (1980). *The Sociology of Youth and Youth Subcultures.* London: Routledge and Kegan Paul.

——— (1985). *Comparative Youth Culture: The Sociology of Youth Cultures and Youth Subcultures in America, Britain and Canada.* London: Routledge and Kegan Paul.

Brewer, D., and M. Miller (1990). "Bombing and Burning: The Social Organization and Values of Hip Hop Graffiti Writers and Implications for Policy." *Deviant Behavior* 11:345–69.

Brooke, M. (1999). *The Concrete Wave: The History of Skateboarding.* Toronto: Warwick Publishing.

Brown, D. (2002). *NOV York: Written by a Slave.* New York: Xlibris.

Brudson, R. (2007). "Police Don't Like Black People: African-American Young Men's Accumulated Police Experiences." *Criminology and Public Policy* 6(1).

Castleman, C. (1982). *Getting Up: Subway Graffiti in New York.* Cambridge: MIT Press.

Chalfant, H., and J. Prigoff (1987). *Spraycan Art.* London: Thames and Hudson.

Chuck D. and Y. Jah (1997). *Fight the Power: Rap, Race, and Reality.* New York: Delacorte Press.

Clifford, J., and G. Marcus, eds. (1986). *Writing Culture: The Poetics and Politics of Ethnography.* Berkeley: University of California Press.

Cloward, R., and L. Ohlin (1961). *Delinquency and Opportunity: A Theory of Delinquent Gangs.* New York: Free Press.

Cohen, A. (1955). *Delinquent Boys: The Culture of the Gang.* New York: Free Press.

——— (1966). *Deviance and Social Control.* Englewood Cliffs, NJ: Prentice-Hall.

Cooper, M., and H. Chalfant (1984). *Subway Art.* London: Thames and Hudson.

Costello, M., and D. Wallace (1989). *Signifying Rappers.* Boston: Ecco Press.

De Certeau, M. (1984). *The Practice of Everyday Life.* Berkeley: University of California Press.

Denzin, N. (1997). *Interpretive Ethnography: Ethnographic Practices for the 21st Century.* Thousand Oaks, CA: Sage.

Denzin, N., and Y. Lincoln, eds. (1994) *Handbook of Qualitative Research.* Thousand Oaks, CA: Sage Publications.

Du Bois, W. E .B, (1969 [1903]) *The Souls of Black Folk.* New York: Signet.

Duncombe, S. (1997). *Notes from Underground: Zines and the Politics of Alternative Culture.* New York: Verso.

Duneier, M. (1999). *Sidewalk*. New York: Farrar, Straus and Giroux.

Dyson, M. (1996). *Between God and Gangster Rap: Bearing Witness to Black Culture*. New York: Oxford University Press.

Eisenstadt, S. N. (1956). *From Generation to Generation*. Chicago: Free Press.

Ellis, C., and A. Bochner (1996) *Composing Ethnography: Alternative Forms of Qualitative Research*. Walnut Creek, CA: AltaMira Press.

Ellis, C., and M. Flaherty, eds. (1992). *Investigating Subjectivity: Research on Lived Experience*. Newbury Park, CA: Sage.

Ferrell, J. (1996). *Crimes of Style: Urban Graffiti and the Politics of Criminality*. Boston: Northeastern University Press.

——— (1998). "Freight Train Graffiti: Subculture, Crime, Dislocation." *Justice Quarterly* 15(4): 587–608.

——— (2001). *Tearing Down the Streets: Adventures in Urban Anarchy*. New York: Palgrave.

——— (2006). *Empire of Scrounge: Inside the Urban Underground of Dumpster Diving, Trash Picking, and Street Scavenging*. New York: New York University Press.

Ferrell, J., et al. (2004). *Cultural Criminology Unleashed*. London: Glasshouse Press.

Ferrell, J., and M. Hamm, eds. (1998). *Ethnography at the Edge*. Boston: Northeastern University Press.

Ferrell, J., D. Milovanovic, and S. Lyng (2001). "Edgework, Media Practices, and the Elongation of Meaning." *Theoretical Criminology* 5(2): 177–202.

Ferrell, J., and C. Sanders, eds. (1995). *Cultural Criminology*. Boston: Northeastern University Press.

Flores, J. (2000). *From Bomba to Hip-Hop: Puerto Rican Culture and Latino Identity*. New York: Columbia University Press.

Forman, M., and M. Neal (2004). *That's the Joint: The Hip Hop Studies Reader*. New York: Routledge.

Foucault, M. (1984). "On the Genealogy of Ethics: An Overview of a Work in Progress." In *The Foucault Reader*, ed. P. Rabinow. New York: Pantheon Books.

Friedman, G. (1994). *Fuck You Heroes: Photographs 1976–1991*. New York: Burning Flags Press.

Gastman, R. (2001). *Free Agents: A History of Washington, D.C. Graffiti*. Bethesda, MD: R. Rock Enterprises.

Geertz, C. (1973). *The Interpretation of Cultures*. New York: Basic Books.

Gelder, K., and S. Thornton, eds. (1997). *The Subcultures Reader*. New York: Routledge.

George, N. (1992). *Elevating the Game: Black Men and Basketball*. New York: HarperCollins.

Goldstein, R. (1980). "In Praise of Graffiti: The Fire Down Below." *Village Voice*, December 24, p. 58.

Goldstein, R. (1998). "Generation Graff: Branded as Young Vandals, Young Graffiti Writers Bomb On." *Village Voice*, January 20, p. 59.

Goldstein, R. (1999a). "The New Real Thing: Barry McGee Throws Up in Soho." *Village Voice*, April 13, p. 41.

——— (1999b). "Rudy's Most Wanted: Stephen Powers Is the Latest Celebrity Quality-of-Life Offender." *Village Voice*, December 21, pp. 66–67.

——— (2000). "The Joy of Bombing: Graffiti's Next Generation Gets Up by Any Means Necessary." *Village Voice*, November 28, pp. 38–40.

Goodall, H. L. (2000). *Writing the New Ethnography*. Walnut Creek, CA: AltaMira Press.

Gwaltney, J. (1983). *Drylongso: A Self-Portrait of Black America*. New York: New Press.

Hager, S. (1984). *Hip Hop: The Illustrated History of Break Dancing, Rap Music and Graffiti*. New York: St. Martin's Press.

Hall, S., and T. Jefferson, eds. (1975). *Resistance through Rituals: Youth Subcultures in Postwar Britain*. London: Hutchinson.

Harper, D. (1987). *Working Knowledge: Skill and Community in a Small Shop*. Chicago: University of Chicago Press.

Hayward, K. (2004). *City Limits: Crime, Consumer Culture and the Urban Experience*. London: Glasshouse Press.

Hebdige, D. (1979). *Subculture: The Meaning of Style*. London: Routledge.

Hodkinson, P. (2002). *Goth: Identity, Style and Subculture*. Oxford: Berg.

Holman-Jones, S. (1998). *Kaleidoscope Notes: Writing Women's Music and Organizational Culture*. Walnut Creek, CA: AltaMira Press.

hooks, b. (1990). *Yearning: Race, Gender and Cultural Politics*. Boston: South End Press.

Hubbard, J., ed. (1994). *Shooting Back from the Reservation: A Photographic View of Life by Native American Youth*. New York: New Press.

Jankowski, M. (1991). *Islands in the Street: Gangs and American Urban Society*. Berkeley: University of California Press.

Karmen, A. (2000). *New York Murder Mystery: The True Story behind the Crime Crash of the 1990s*. New York: New York University Press.

Katz, J. (1988). *Seductions of Crime*. New York: Basic Books.

Kelley, R. (1997). *Yo Mama's Dysfunctional: Fighting the Culture Wars in Urban America*. New York: Beacon Press.

Kitwana, B. (1994). *The Rap on Gangsta Rap*. Chicago: Third World Press.

——— (2004). *Why Whites Kids Love Hip Hop: Wiggers, Wangstas and Wannabees*. New York: Basic Civitas Books.

Klein, N. (2000). *No Logo*. New York: Picador.

Kohl, H. (1972). "Names, Graffiti and Culture," in *Rappin' and Stylin' Out: Communication in Urban Black America*, ed. T. Kochman. Urbana: University of Illinois Press.

Kohl, H., with photographs by J. Hinton (1972). *Golden Boy as Anthony Cool.* New York: Dial Press.

Krieger, S. (1991). *Social Science and the Self: Personal Essays on an Artform.* New Brunswick, NJ: Rutgers University Press.

Kurlansky, M. (1974). *The Faith of Graffiti.* Documented by Mervyn Kurlansky and Jon Naar. Text by Norman Mailer. New York: Praeger.

Lachmann, R. (1988). "Graffiti as Career and Ideology." *American Journal of Sociology* 94(2): 229–50.

Lareau, A., and J. Shultz, eds. (1996). *Journeys through Ethnography: Realistic Accounts of Fieldwork.* Boulder, CO: Westview Press.

Lefebvre, H. (1974). *The Production of Space.* London: Wiley.

Lemert, E. (1951). *Social Pathology.* New York: McGraw-Hill.

Levy, A. (2007). "Chasing Dash Snow." *New York Magazine,* January 15.

Lipsitz, G. (1994). *Dangerous Crossroads: Popular Music, Postmodernism and the Poetics of Place.* New York: Verso.

Lueck, Thomas. (2006). "Graffiti Back in the Subways, Indelibly This Time." *New York Times,* April 25.

Macdonald, N. (2001). *The Graffiti Subculture: Youth, Masculinity and Identity in London and New York.* London: Palgrave.

MacLeod, J. (1995). *Ain't No Makin' It: Aspirations and Attainment in a Low-Income Neighborhood.* Boulder, CO: Westview Press.

Maffesoli, M. (1996). *The Times of the Tribes: The Decline of Individualism in Mass Society.* Thousand Oaks, CA: Sage.

Males, M. (1996a). *Framing Youth.* Monroe, ME: Common Courage Press.

——— (1996b). *The Scapegoat Generation: America's War on Adolescents.* Monroe, ME: Common Courage Press.

Manning, P., and M. Truzzi, eds. (1972). *Youth and Sociology.* Englewood Cliffs, NJ: Prentice-Hall.

Marcus, Greil (1990). *Lipstick Traces: A Secret History of the 20th Century.* Cambridge: Harvard University Press.

Marcus, George (1998). *Ethnography through Thick and Thin.* Princeton: Princeton University Press.

Marx, K. (1978 [1848]). "The Communist Manifesto." In *The Marx-Engels Reader,* ed. Robert C. Tucker. New York: W. W. Norton.

McCracken, G. (1998). *Culture and Consumption: New Approaches to the Symbolic Character of Consumer Goods and Activities.* Bloomington: Indiana University Press.

McRobbie, A., ed. (1988). *Zoot Suits and Second Hand Dresses: An Anthology of Fashion and Music.* Boston: Unwin Hyman.

——— (1991). *Feminism and Youth Culture: From "Jackie" to "Just Seventeen."* Boston: Unwin Hyman.

McRobbie, A., ed. (1999). *In the Culture of Society: Art, Fashion, and Popular Music.* New York: Routledge.

Merton, R. (1938). "Social Structure and Anomie." *American Sociological Review* 3:672–82.

Miller, I. (1991). "Night Train: The Power That Man Made." *New York Folklore* 17(1–2): 21–43.

——— (1994). "Piecing: The Dynamics of Style." *Calligraphy Review* 11(1): 20–33.

——— (2002). *Aerosol Kingdom: Subway Painters of New York City.* Jackson: University Press of Mississippi.

Morton, M. (1995). *The Tunnel.* New Haven: Yale University Press.

Muggleton, D. (2000). *Inside Subculture: The Postmodern Meaning of Style.* London: Berg.

Muggleton, D., and R. Weinzierl, eds. (2003). *The Post-Subcultures Reader.* London: Berg.

Parenti, C. (1996). *Lockdown America: Police and Prisons in an Age of Crisis.* New York: Verso.

Parsons, T. (1963). "Youth in the Context of American Society." In *Social Structure and Personality.* New York: Free Press.

Phillips, S. (1999). *Wallbangin': Graffiti and Gangs in L.A.* Chicago: University of Chicago Press.

Polsky, N. (1969). *Hustlers, Beats, and Others.* New York: Anchor Books.

Potter, R. (1995). *Spectacular Vernaculars: Hip-Hop and the Politics of Post-Modernism.* Albany: State University of New York Press.

Powers, S. (1999). *The Art of Getting Over: Graffiti at the Millennium.* New York: St. Martin's Press.

——— (2005). *First and Fifteenth: Pop Art Short Stories.* New York: Villard Books.

Pressler, J. (2006). "Remember Zines? Look at Them Now." *New York Times,* May 7, sec. 9, p. 14.

Reed-Danahay, D., ed. (1997). *Auto/Ethnography: Rewriting the Self and the Social.* New York. Berg.

Richardson, L. (1990). *Writing Strategies.* Newbury Park, CA: Sage.

Rose, A., and C. Strike, eds. (2004). *Beautiful Losers: Contemporary Art and Street Culture.* New York: Iconoclast.

Rose, D. (1987). *Black American Street Life: South Philadelphia, 1969–1971.* Philadelphia: University of Pennsylvania Press.

——— (1990). *Living the Ethnographic Life.* Newbury Park, CA: Sage.

Rose, T. (1994). *Black Noise: Rap Music and Black Culture in Contemporary America.* Middletown, CT: Wesleyan University Press.

Ross, A., and T. Rose, eds. (1994). *Microphone Fiends: Youth Music and Youth Culture.* New York: Routledge.

Schmidlapp, D., and Phase 2 (1996). *Style: Writing from the Underground; (R)evolutions of Aerosol Linguistics*. Terni, Italy: Stampa Alternativa in Association with IGTimes.

Seale, B. (1991 [1971]). *Seize the Time: The Story of the Black Panther Party and Huey P. Newton*. New York: Black Classic Press.

Shakur, S. [Monster Kody Scott] (1994). *The Life of an L.A. Gang Member*. New York: Penguin.

Siegel, N. (1999). "From the Subways to the Streets." *New York Times*, August 22.

Simmel, G. (1971). "The Conflict in Modern Culture." In *On Individuality and Social Forms*. Chicago: University of Chicago Press.

Stack, C. (1974). *All our Kin: Strategies for Survival in a Black Community*. New York: Harper and Row.

Stewart, J. (1989). "Subway Graffiti: An Aesthetic Study of Graffiti on the Subway System of New York City, 1970–1978." Ph.D. Diss. New York University.

Stringer, L. (1998). *Grand Central Winter*. New York: Seven Stories Press.

Sutherland, P. (2004). *Autograf: New York City's Graffiti Writers*. Text by REVS. New York: Powerhouse Books.

Thornton, S. (1996). *Club Cultures: Music, Media and Subcultural Capital*. Cambridge: Polity Press.

Toop, D. (1984). *The Rap Attack: African Jive to New York Hip-Hop*. London: South End Press.

——— (1992). *Rap Attack 2*. Boston: Consortium Press.

Toth, J. (1993). *The Mole People: Life in the Tunnels beneath New York City*. Chicago: Chicago Review Press.

Van Maanen, J. (1988). *Tales of the Field: On Writing Ethnography*. Chicago: University of Chicago Press.

Wacquant, L. (2004). *Body and Soul: Notes from an Apprentice Boxer*. New York: Oxford University Press.

Walker, R. (2005). "Slicker Price." *New York Times*, October 30.

Walsh, M. (1996). *Graffito*. San Francisco: North Atlantic Books.

West, C. (1994). *Race Matters*. New York: Vintage Books.

Whyte, W. (1973 [1947]). *Street Corner Society*. Chicago: University of Chicago Press.

Williams, T. (1989). *Cocaine Kids: The Inside Story of a Teenage Drug Ring*. New York: Addison-Wesley.

——— (1992). *Crackhouse: Notes from the End of the Line*. New York: Addison-Wesley.

Williams, T., and W. Kornblum. (1985). *Growing Up Poor*. Lexington, MA: D. C. Heath.

——— (1994). *The Uptown Kids: Struggle and Hope in the Projects*. New York: G. P. Putnam and Sons.

Willis, P. (1977). *Learning to Labour: How Working-Class Kids Get Working-Class Jobs*. London: Saxon House.

Wilson, J., and G. Kelling (1982). "Broken Windows: Police and Neighborhood Safety." *Atlantic Monthly*, March, pp. 29–38.

Wimsatt, W. (1994). *Bomb the Suburbs*. Chicago: Subway and Elevated Press.

——— (1999). *No More Prisons*. New York: Softskull Press.

Witten, A., and M. White (2001). *Dondi White: Style Master General*. New York: Regan Books.

GRAFFITI MAGAZINES

Mass Appeal
While You Were Sleeping
On the Go
Big Time
Flashbacks
BackJumps
12oz. Prophet

SKATEBOARD MAGAZINES

Transworld
Thrasher
Big Brother
Slap
411 Video Magazine

FILMS

Wild Style (1983). Directed by Charlie Ahearn.
Style Wars (1983). Directed by Henry Chalfant and Tony Silver.
The Show (1995). Directed by Brian Robbins.
Beat Street (1984). Directed by Stan Lathan.
Krush Groove (1985). Directed by Michael Schultz.
Breakin' (1984). Directed by Joel Silberg.
Quadrophenia (1979). Directed by Franc Roddam.
Sid and Nancy (1986). Directed by Alex Cox.
The Filth and the Fury (2000). Directed by Julien Temple.

ONLINE RESOURCES

www.graffiti.org
robotswillkill.com
saster.net (Streets Are Saying Things)

INDEX

The names of graffiti writers appear in SMALL CAPS.
Page numbers in *italics* refer to illustrations on that page.

About the Author

Gregory J. Snyder is Assistant Professor of Sociology and Anthropology at Baruch College, City University of New York.